BUSHCRAFT SKILLS
AND HOW TO SURVIVE IN THE WILD

BUSHCRAFT SKILLS
AND HOW TO SURVIVE IN THE WILD
A STEP-BY-STEP PRACTICAL GUIDE

A complete handbook to wilderness survival – all the knowledge and expertise you need
for preserving life in extreme conditions, with over 650 photographs and illustrations

ANTHONIO AKKERMANS

southwater

This edition is published by Southwater, an imprint of
Anness Publishing Ltd, Hermes House, 88–89 Blackfriars Road
London SE1 8HA; tel. 020 7401 2077; fax 020 7633 9499

www.southwaterbooks.com; www.annesspublishing.com

If you like the images in this book and would like to investigate using them
for publishing, promotions or advertising, please visit our website
www.practicalpictures.com for more information.

UK agent: The Manning Partnership Ltd
tel. 01225 478444; fax 01225 478440; sales@manning-partnership.co.uk
UK distributor: Grantham Book Services Ltd
tel. 01476 541080; fax 01476 541061; orders@gbs.tbs-ltd.co.uk
North American agent/distributor: National Book Network
tel. 301 459 3366; fax 301 429 5746; www.nbnbooks.com
Australian agent/distributor: Pan Macmillan Australia
tel. 1300 135 113; fax 1300 135 103; customer.service@macmillan.com.au
New Zealand agent/distributor: David Bateman Ltd
tel. (09) 415 7664; fax (09) 415 8892

Publisher: Joanna Lorenz
Editorial Director: Helen Sudell
Editors: Sarah Ainley, James Harrison and Elizabeth Woodland
Photography: Helen Metcalfe and Tim Gundry
Illustrations: Patrick Mulrey and Peter Bull Studios
Designer: Nigel Partridge
Cover Designer: Nigel Partridge
Editorial Reader: Jay Thundercliffe
Production Controller: Wendy Lawson

Ethical Trading Policy

At Anness Publishing we believe that business should be conducted in an
ethical and ecologically sustainable way, with respect for the environment
and a proper regard to the replacement of the natural resources we employ.
As a publisher, we use a lot of wood pulp to make high-quality paper for
printing, and that wood commonly comes from spruce trees. We are
therefore currently growing more than 500,000 trees in two Scottish forest
plantations near Aberdeen – Berrymoss (130 hectares/320 acres) and West
Touxhill (125 hectares/305 acres). The forests we manage contain twice the
number of trees employed each year in paper-making for our books.
Because of this ongoing ecological investment programme, you, as our
customer, can have the pleasure and reassurance of knowing that a tree is
being cultivated on your behalf to naturally replace the materials used to
make the book you are holding.
Our forestry programme is run in accordance with the UK Woodland
Assurance Scheme (UKWAS) and will be certified by the internationally
recognized Forest Stewardship Council (FSC). The FSC is a non-
government organization dedicated to promoting responsible management
of the world's forests. Certification ensures forests are managed in an
environmentally sustainable and socially responsible way. For further
information about this scheme, go to www.annesspublishing.com/trees

© Anness Publishing Ltd 2007

Previously published as part of a larger volume, *Extreme Survival*

Publisher's Warning

CONTENTS

INTRODUCTION
by Debra Searle MBE

Survival is necessary only when the environment becomes unfamiliar to us and we are far beyond our comfort zone, battling with situations outside the realms of our previous experience.

THE WILL TO SURVIVE
Over the years much research has been conducted into why it should be that some people can survive a life-threatening situation when others in the same situation are overwhelmed. Often it is not the strongest or those with the best equipment who make it, although these things undoubtedly make a big difference. Unequivocally, the same conclusion is always reached: the difference between living or dying

▼ *Debra Searle has honed her mental survival skills both as a sports psychologist and as an extreme sports participator.*

lies in the mind. The power of the mind, the resilience of the human spirit, an unshakable optimism and a mental readiness to handle the unexpected are vital in the ultimate survival situations.

Naturally some people have these qualities in abundance, but not all. Happily there are skills that can be learned to help us achieve the necessary mental strength. Just as we can repeat movements, like the running action or biceps curl, to make our bodies physically fitter, so the same principle can also be applied to the mind. But as with getting our bodies fitter, we have to work at it and repeat the action to increase our performance.

The two most important mental strength-building skills that can be developed can be summed up in two words – visualization and attitude.

VISUALIZATION
It may sound like psychobabble at first, but visualization is certainly not just for elite athletes. The idea is that by mentally imagining doing an action we can train our bodies to carry out that action without actually moving or completing it for real; therefore a thought alone can produce a physical response. An example of this that we can all experience is imagining sucking on a slice of lemon. When we do we get a rush of saliva to the mouth yet there is not a real lemon in sight! Our minds have just induced a physical response to the thought. Visualization is the most powerful survival tool we can ever develop because often we cannot replicate an actual situation in order to practise surviving. However, if we can use our minds to rehearse mentally how we will respond, our

▶ *Bushcraft skills can employ modern tools like a well-designed steel utility knife, but should also be based upon utilizing – and respecting – what nature has to offer.*

minds and bodies will be trained and automatically know what to do if and when the situation arises.

Not only can visualization help us achieve the right physical response, it is also incredibly powerful for eliminating fear. Let's face it – any survival situation is likely to be terrifying, but if we can remain calm we are likely to be able to analyse, prioritize and plan a response amid the chaos and confusion. When visualization is used in this way it is like watching a scary movie for the second time. The first time you put the DVD in the machine and press Play you find yourself jumping at the scary bits because you don't quite know when they are going to happen. But when you put the DVD in for a second viewing and press Play you don't jump when you get to the scary bits, because you have seen it all before and know that it is coming.

We often feel fear because we don't know what is going to happen next, but if we can visualize some of the possibilities by running our own "movies" in our heads we can eliminate some of the fear. We simply press Play when the situation arises.

THE POWER OF VISUALIZATION

Perhaps one of the most powerful ways to use visualization is as a means of developing that eternal optimism and hardness of human spirit that is so vital for survival. It is also possibly the simplest form of visualization to develop, for all you really need to do is visualize that one thing that is worth living for.

We all have something to live for – something we love more than anything else. Maybe it would be to hold your child again, drive your car, watch your favourite football team win a home game... Whatever it may be you just have to visualize it using every sense in your body and imagine how amazing it will feel to do that again.

CHOOSE YOUR ATTITUDE

The one element common to many of the scenarios in this book is that we don't have a choice about being in these life-threatening situations. We can attempt to avoid them but some are unavoidable. For example, we have little choice about being involved in a kidnap, a terrorist attack or a natural disaster. Often the situation will be totally out of our control. If this is the case then it is vital to be able to recognize those things that you do have a choice about, rather than wasting time and energy worrying about those things that you have no control over. You may not be able to change the situation but you can always change the way in which you are responding to it. You can always "choose your attitude".

"Choose your attitude" is more than just a motto – it is a way of life.

So as you read this book, don't just let the words flow over you. Instead, visualize yourself in the situation and imagine how you would respond. Live the survival situation now in the safety of your own home, just in case you ever have to face it for real. And remember: choose your attitude.

THE KEYS TO SURVIVAL

What do we need most to survive? Many people will answer "food", when asked about what they feel is a priority in a survival situation. It makes sense that we should think this way, because, of the four basic requirements for life, we can take three of them for granted in our modern lifestyle.

Water comes from the tap on demand, our houses are our shelters from the elements, and few of us need to light a fire when we feel cold. Food is the only need we put more thought into. We cook every evening, and we notice instantly when food runs out. However, we can actually survive for a long time without food. It is water intake that is vital, because without water we would die in three to five days.

This book looks at the principles of bushcraft and the four cornerstones of survival. It shows you how to ensure that you can live in a hostile wilderness environment by building a shelter, making fires, finding food and water and keeping yourself safe.

PRINCIPLES OF BUSHCRAFT

Learning bushcraft skills allows us to live off the land naturally, travel light, and survive most terrain when equipment is scarce or not available. Even if we are not in a survival situation, bushcraft skills provide a profound way of connecting with our ancestors and allowing us to revive our link with the earth. In fact, bushcraft skills are really earth-living skills, managing without modern tools or aids. Acquiring these skills requires diligent practice and maintenance, but once learned they open a world of possibilities. Most importantly, these skills belong to anyone and have been passed on by those who travelled the wilderness trails before us. They should be preserved intact for the next generation.

Mental and emotional survival

By far the biggest problem people face when thrust into a survival situation is not how to find food or water, but how to cope mentally with the situation. Suddenly they have to rely on their instincts, and a whole range of powerful and conflicting emotions can surface. Psychologists generally agree that there is a classic sequence of reactions to any traumatic event: shock, denial, fear and anger, blame, depression, acceptance, and moving on – or variations of those emotions.

EMOTIONAL RESPONSES
• **Shock** You are unprepared for what's just hit you. You have difficulty processing the information.
• **Denial** As a survival mechanism, you may now acknowledge your situation, but you refuse to believe it is true. You continue to say, "No, this can't be happening to me."
• **Anger** You become enraged over your situation. You are upset that things aren't the way they were, and you're scared that you'll never get back to normal.
• **Blame** Blaming others for your

▼ *The most inhospitable environment can yield clues for survival. Green shrubbery indicates a water source in a desert.*

situation makes you feel better but makes little rational sense.
• **Depression** This is internalized anger. You search for some way to make your stress more manageable.
• **Acceptance** Now you are getting "real". You are facing reality, however wild and remote it appears to be.
• **Moving on** Mentally you begin to

▲ *Solve each problem as it arises. Once a problem has been fully resolved, you are free to move on to the next issue.*

redress the balance and think about your situation and how you are going to survive, not just for the next few hours but the next few days and weeks.

DON'T PANIC
In a survival situation, feelings of helplessness can turn into depression and loneliness very quickly. One of the greatest and most difficult emotional states to deal with is panic. Panic can cause you to perform irrational actions that can worsen the situation you're in. In extreme circumstances, failure to remain calm can even endanger your life, just because you didn't have the presence of mind to make the right decisions. Most of the time, you won't even realize you're panicking.

The first step to beating panic is to recognize the fact that you may panic if you don't take steps to prevent it. When you are in an unnerving situation it is important to take things step by step and to give yourself a chance to assess your situation properly.

ONE STEP AT A TIME

Don't fall into the trap of adding all your problems one on top of the other until they become one gigantic problem. Sit down for a moment, take a few deep breaths, and think about your most urgent difficulty. Then concentrate on solving this particular problem. After this first issue is resolved, you can move on to the next. Take it one step at a time.

There is an apt story of the man who found himself having to paddle a kayak back to shore during a storm on the ocean. If this man had thought about all the waves he would have to survive, he might well have drowned. Instead, he took it one wave at a time, taking care to steer his kayak right into each wave as it came and never thinking about the next problem until the current one was solved. He battled against the waves for hours, but made it to calmer waters and the shore in the end.

STAYING UPBEAT IS A SKILL

Many people feel that maintaining an upbeat mentality is something you read about and then remember when it really matters. This isn't the case.

Controlling your mindset is as much a skill as making fire by friction. You can practise your mental skills by applying a calm, positive approach to events in your everyday life. Whenever things start to get tough, just do one thing and then turn to the next on the list. Not only will this prepare you for any survival situation, you will also find that it makes day-to-day life a lot more enjoyable and less stressful.

You can ensure an upbeat mentality by making sure you have the skills to provide for yourself and others. Well-honed skills will boost your confidence and will help keep panic at bay.

SURVIVAL IN A GROUP

There is safety in numbers and obvious physical advantages in having someone else there if you are injured or weak. But there are other advantages to being in a group when you are in a survival situation. The greatest is that there are more individuals to take care of the necessary tasks of day-to-day living. Not only do many hands make light work, but the various individuals in the party are bound to have different strengths and weaknesses. If you are

▲ *In a survival situation with another person or a group, a lot of emotional comfort can be shared between individuals.*

someone who is very good at building a shelter but less proficient at finding wild edibles, for instance, being part of a group allows you to put all your efforts into providing an effective group shelter, while feeling secure that other people in the group will provide other necessities, such as food, water and fire.

There are also a few disadvantages, however. Now you have to provide not only for yourself, but for the whole group. If all the other group members have a certain amount of outdoor skills and there are plenty of resources around, this may not be a difficulty, but if you are the only one with any survival skills or if there aren't many supplies available, it can be very hard to ensure that the whole group is well hydrated, fed and comfortable. It may also happen that one member of the group is injured and needs taking care of. After all, the chain is only as strong as its weakest link.

SURVIVING ALONE

If you are on your own, one of the most difficult problems to overcome is loneliness, which can quickly lead to feelings of hopelessness, panic and then desperation. To counteract this, use visualization skills to overcome fears. Imagine yourself rescued and work towards making that happen. Make a list of priorities and stick to it. Keep focused on the task in hand and drive away negative thoughts whenever they creep into your head. Take strength from each task you complete. A strong mental attitude will pull you through.

GROUP PRIORITIES

Follow these steps to ensure that your group is well prepared to face the challenges ahead.

- Choose a leader. This should be the person with the greatest skill, who must be able to carry the responsibility, acting as chairperson rather than as dictator. As leader, you must take responsibility for the situation and organize any tasks that need to be completed; listen to all the ideas the group bring forward and help them come to any decisions that need to be made. Sometimes this may not be possible, and you will have to make decisions and assign tasks, for instance in the case that only one of your group has the relevant knowledge.
- List all the tasks needed to ensure immediate survival and share them out among the group members.

- Find out what each individual's strong points are, so that tasks can be put in the most able hands. Some tasks will have to be done by everyone working together, such as building the group shelter.
- Keep each other up to date on the progress the group is making, and make sure everybody is still OK. Promote a feeling of mutual dependence within the group, so that everyone is there for the whole group and no one feels left out. Make sure that people who have difficulty with certain tasks get help.
- Make an inventory of all the items in everyone's possession. In the case of a crash, try to rescue as much from the wreckage as possible: anything from electrical wires (to use as cordage) to the stuffing in the seats (for insulation).

Signalling for help

It cannot be stressed enough that whenever you go on a trip in the wilderness people back home should know where you're headed and what time you expect to arrive at your destination. This way there will be people in the outside world who will miss you (and your fellow travellers) if something does go wrong.

If you have found yourself (alone or with a group) in a survival situation and it was not by choice – if your vehicle has crashed, for instance – there is another issue to consider. With every decision you make, whether it is in siting your camp or leaving it to find food and water, you need to ensure that any rescue teams who reach the area will be able to find you.

LEAVING SIGNS FOR RESCUERS

It is all too common for people to leave a crash site without any indication where they were headed. It is best to remain near the crash site, but if the site cannot sustain you it may sometimes be necessary to move away. In this case, it is vital that you leave

clear signs behind, indicating the number of survivors, whether any are wounded and where you have gone.

Once you have arrived at a site that can sustain you well and you decide to settle and wait for rescue, make sure your site is clearly visible from the air. You can do this by making large signs on the ground with sticks or any other easily distinguishable material. If a sign is at any distance from the actual camp, make sure it indicates where the camp is by means of an arrow.

Another idea is to throw green plants and leaves on to the camp fire during the day, as smoke is a good indicator of where you are. During the

▼ *If you draw signs on a beach it is very important that they are above the high tide mark, so they are not washed away in the surf. Rather than drawing in the sand, use rocks or branches, which show up clearly.*

▲ *Using stones, you can lay out signs on or beside the trail for rescuers to follow. These signs are mainly useful when leaving the site of an accident.*

night you may want to have a large fire, depending on your resources. If you have got plenty of fuel, one thing you can do is to construct three fires in a triangle with the corners approximately 10m/33ft apart.

▼ *When abandoning a crash site you must leave signs that make it clear there are survivors, and show where you have gone.*

LEAVING TRAIL SIGNS

	STRAIGHT AHEAD	TURN RIGHT	TURN LEFT	DO NOT GO THIS WAY
ROCKS				
PEBBLES				
STICKS				
LONG GRASS				
NUMBER OF PACES IN DIRECTION INDICATED		I HAVE GONE HOME		

There are many ways to leave tell-tale signs for would-be rescuers that you have passed by this trail and to show your onward direction. Use rocks if possible, otherwise wood or even rooted grass and foliage.

ESSENTIAL SIGNALLING TO AN AIRCRAFT

▲ Stretch out both arms as if to embrace the aircraft to ask the crew to fly towards you to pick you up.

▲ Stretch out both arms sideways, to signal to the pilot to hold the aircraft in a hover pattern.

▲ Palms down, arms outstretched, moving your arm up like a bird's wings, tells the aircraft to descend.

▲ Lower your outstretched arm as part of the bird-like movement to make it clear to the pilot it's safe to descend.

▲ With left arm outstretched, wave your right arm to make it clear that the pilot needs to move to your left.

▲ Continue waving your right arm deliberately and keep your left arm outstretched to maintain this signal.

▲ Placing both hands behind your ears indicates that your receiver is working.

▲ This signal indicates to the pilot that mechanical aid is needed.

▲ This tells the pilot that the safe direction to exit is to your left.

▲ Stretch out your arms in a particular direction and bend your knees, to show the area that is a safe landing zone.

▲ Moving both outstretched arms parallel above you from side to side says: "Do not try to land."

▲ Stretching your arms out in front of you and waving them up and down signals the word "yes".

Finding your bearings

Getting your bearings is essential for survival in the wild – that doesn't just mean finding the direction of north or south but, rather, being aware of your surroundings. As one wilderness instructor has put it: "You cannot get lost unless you have a place to go to and a time to be there." There is good sense in this saying.

In many cases when you accidentally find yourself in a survival situation, you may not know exactly where you are. You may not know what civilization lies closest to you. In such instances, knowing where north or south is may not really be an advantage. It is more important to learn as much as you can about your surroundings. Find a stream or river and follow it down – you will

often come to some sort of civilization this way. You may also want to listen very carefully for any sounds of modern day life, such as trains, factories or traffic noise.

If you do need to establish the direction, it can be time-consuming if you have to rely solely on natural resources. There may be times when it is simply impossible to say for sure which way you're facing. For example, though it is often true that mosses grow on the north side of trees, it is not always the case – moss can grow all around a tree, so it is not a very good idea to rely on this kind of method. However, there are some techniques that can work for you if you need to find the cardinal directions.

NAVIGATIONAL STARS

North Star Also known as Polaris or the Pole Star and located above the North Pole, it is a key reference for north. It is the only star that appears to remain static in the sky.
The Plough Also known as the Big Dipper, it forms part of the large Great Bear constellation.
Orion Also known as the Hunter, this rises above the equator and can be seen in both hemispheres.
Southern Cross This indicates south in the southern hemisphere.
Milky Way A hazy band of stars stretching across the sky. The dark patch in it is called the Coalsack.

DIRECTION-FINDING WITH A SHADOW STICK

1 If you don't have a compass you can use the sun to get your bearings. Find a stick at least 50cm/20in long and drive it vertically into flat, even ground.

2 Find a number of small pebbles, and place one on the tip of the shadow the stick is casting on the ground. Now wait 10–20 minutes.

3 You will find that the tip of the shadow has moved. Take another pebble and place this where the tip of the shadow now reaches.

4 Wait another 10–20 minutes. The shadow of the stick will have moved even farther round. Take a third pebble and once again place it on the tip of the shadow.

5 The pebbles you have placed on the ground will form a line. This line goes from east to west. To find the north-south axis, place a stick at right angles to the line of pebbles.

6 This stick will point north and south. If you follow the direction of the stick with the sun at your back, you will be walking north; walking towards the sun will take you south.

USING THE STARS TO FIND DIRECTION

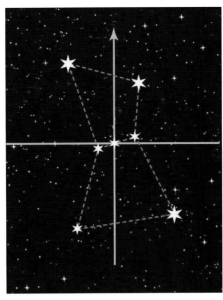

▲ *The North Star lies above the North Pole and can be found by running a line into the sky from the far side of the Plough's pan.*

▲ *An imaginary line drawn across the middle of Orion lies roughly east–west in the northern hemisphere.*

▲ *The Southern Cross will help you to find south in the southern hemisphere. Note the false cross of dimmer stars to the right.*

▲ *Keep a button compass handy as part of your travel kit for emergencies. It will pinpoint your direction accurately.*

FINDING NORTH BY THE STARS

To find a northerly direction in the northern hemisphere on a clear night, look for the constellation of the Plough or Big Dipper and draw an imaginary line from the two stars farthest from the "handle". This line will intersect with the North Star, also known as the Pole Star (five times the distance between the two "guiding" stars). Once you have located the North Star, push a stick in the ground then insert a second stick, lined up so that when you look over the first stick you can see the second one

directly under Polaris. If you leave the two sticks in the ground, they will act as a reminder of the direction in daylight.

In the southern hemisphere, the best celestial signpost is the Southern Cross, which circles the South Pole. This constellation, located near the dark area known as the Coalsack in the Milky Way, has four bright stars in the shape of a cross and two "pointer" stars beside it. Imagine a line through the longer part of the cross and another line bisecting the two bright pointer stars – these two lines intersect at the celestial South Pole.

USING THE SUN TO MEASURE TIME

1 To see how much light is left, extend your arm towards the sun. Each finger's width represents about 20 minutes.

2 Bend your wrist so your hand is horizontal and lower your hand so that it appears to "rest" on the horizon.

3 The sun is visible above three fingers. This means that it is about one hour after sunrise or before sunset.

Taking care of yourself and others

Although you should learn how to do without it, it is advisable to carry a small survival kit with you at all times. A few basic items will make some tasks a bit easier for you or allow you to get vital chores done using less energy.

ESSENTIAL SURVIVAL KIT

A knife will be your most useful tool in most survival situations, but the other items listed here won't take up much space and could be very helpful.

• Penknife
• Waterproof matches
• Candle
• Fishing line
• Fish hooks of various sizes
• Two small fishing lures
• Snare wire
• Water purifying tablets
• Whistle
• Cord
• Safety pins/needles
• Surgical adhesive tape
• Sticking plasters (Band-Aids)
• Dental floss or strong thread
• Compass
• Tweezers
• Paracetamol (acetaminophen)

Pack these into a small tin (which can also act as a pot to boil water) and seal it with duct tape to keep it dry. Keep your survival kit in your backpack or in your jacket on every trip.

▲ *If you take care in picking the items for your survival kit, they should all fit into a container small enough to fit in a pocket. Take items that you would find hard to make alternatives for in the wild, such as a sharp knife, waterproof matches, a candle, a whistle, safety pins, a needle and strong thread, a hook, some wire and a compass.*

PREVENTION IS BETTER THAN CURE

Common sense will tell you that the best way to treat illness or injury is to prevent it. You don't want to wound yourself by being careless with a knife, for instance, especially when in an accidental survival situation, since adding to your problems will cause your situation to deteriorate faster.

There are a few important guidelines you should follow when out in the wild. The most important is to wash your hands thoroughly after going to the toilet. In a survival situation, a lot of tasks will be done with your bare hands (such as skinning wildlife or gathering water) and you must avoid

any cross-contamination, which could make you or others in your party ill.

Ensure that sharp implements are used and stored correctly so you don't accidentally stab yourself. When using tools such as knives or axes, it is vital that your body is never in the path of the tool or a splinter of stone or metal.

▼ *Take a first-aid course before you go on a major trip or trek. It will help you to assess a survival situation coolly and clearly.*

◄ *Avoid situations that might create self-inflicted injuries, such as lifting too much at once, or placing your feet without looking.*

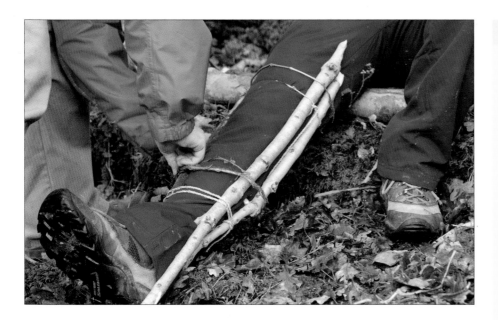

When gathering wood, never break branches over your knee or by jumping on them. It is easy to underestimate the strength of the wood and hurt yourself. Always do the work with sharp tools or by burning them to the right length in a fire (which is a more efficient use of your energy anyway).

Be careful where you put your feet when hiking, and take as little risk as

▲ *When bleeding is controlled and shock has been dealt with, it is time to tend to non-life-threatening wounds like fractures.*

possible. Sometimes it's better to go around difficult terrain than to cross it. Safety should always be uppermost in your mind when there is no one on hand to give you medical treatment if you are ill or injured.

▲ *When you are shaping wood, carve smoothly and slowly, with the blade facing away from your body.*

▲ *Never turn the blade of the knife towards your hand or body, and make sure the path of the knife is clear of obstruction.*

▲ *Never break a branch of wood over your knee in case it is stronger than it looks and you hurt your leg.*

▲ *Jumping on a piece of wood could damage your ankle. If you can't cut it, burn it through to achieve the correct length.*

RESPECTING NATURE

There is a balance to strike between reducing your impact on the environment as much as possible, and staying alive. For example, if your life is not in immediate danger, you can build your shelter using only dead material, but if your life depends on it the conservation rules have to give way. If you have to survive the night and there is not enough debris to shelter you, you shouldn't hesitate to cut down live branches and leaves to use as insulation.

In a non-life-threatening situation, it is important to take care of the environment you live in. You do not, for instance, have to eat every single bulrush or cattail root. Approach your environment much as a gardener would. If you have to cut down particular trees or plants for use in your shelter or for other purposes, always try to find those trees that are in competition with others, so that your action benefits them. Try to pick trees and plants growing in places where they seem less likely to thrive. This kind of "caretaker" attitude could actually improve the area where you find yourself.

A second important rule is not to harvest any plants or kill any animals in the immediate vicinity of your camp. Move at least 100m/110yd away from your camp before looking for what you need. This way, you are not only leaving your immediate area intact, you are also creating an emergency cache. If you were to fall ill, it would be a relief to find edible plants growing right outside your shelter. Always follow a different path to and from your camp, making sure you don't trample too much brush.

If survival forces you to kill an animal for food then use everything there is to glean from that particular animal – meat for food, bones for tools, hide for clothing – leaving nothing to waste.

Natural hazards

Wherever you are in the wild, it is important to watch out for dangerous animals and habitats. The general rule is to be wary at all times.

AVOIDING DANGEROUS WILDLIFE

You actually need to alert potentially dangerous animals of your presence and should certainly not surprise them. Use whistles or bang tins to let them know you are there. They won't want anything to do with you, provided you don't threaten them or their young. It's only the presence of food that may make them view you as a competitor.

When you enter bear country you threaten the animals' status at the top of the food chain. They have an acute sense of smell, so an obvious precaution is to hide food and waste well away from your camp. Keep food at least 300m/330yd from your sleeping area

ESCAPING QUICKSAND

In tropical conditions walk with a strong stick or pole – then if you sink in quicksand (sand saturated in water), you can lie on your back on the pole and "relax". Keep your hips on the pole and your body will float as it is less dense than the sand. If you struggle you will sink deeper. Quicksand is rarely deeper than a few feet. Spread yourself out and backreach for dry land.

tied up in a bear baggy. Burn all toilet paper and feminine hygiene products. Bury your waste at least 15-20cm/6-8in deep.

TICKS AND OTHER INSECTS

Insects can be very harmful. In the tropics, mosquitoes are mainly responsible for passing on illnesses, but even in temperate regions there are insects that can pass on viruses and infections. The most common (and most often ignored) danger in temperate climates comes from ticks. They carry various diseases but Lyme disease is the one to watch out for. In most places the risk is low, but up to one third of ticks in the USA carry it.

Once on your body, the tick will dig into your skin to feed on your blood. After about 12 hours it will release its barb by injecting saliva to dissolve the tissue around the bite. It is this saliva that may contain bacteria or viruses.

If you contract Lyme disease you may or may not find a "bull's-eye-like" rash, which is usually not itchy, and you may have flu-like symptoms such as headache, fever, stiff neck and sore joints. If the infection spreads, it can affect the heart, nervous system and joints. If untreated, it could go on to affect your short-term memory and ultimately be fatal. Treatment is with antibiotics; there is no vaccine.

Remove a tick as soon as you spot it and don't leave it to fall off by itself. In

▼ *Well-camouflaged crocodiles are ambush hunters and kill by gripping, rolling and drowning their victims back in the water.*

BEAR RESPONSES

If confronted by a bear, remain calm and quiet, fall to the ground and protect your neck and stomach by clasping your hands over your neck, and laying face down. Playing dead during an attack has been documented in survival cases. Climbing a tree is not a good option. Grizzly bears can stand over 2m/8ft on their hind legs and climb trees. Fighting back is a last resort.

high-risk areas, check for ticks every 12 hours. Burning it off with a cigarette will only encourage the tick to inject saliva. Instead, grab it with tweezers and pull it straight out.

▼ *Remove leeches with a hot flame or salt. Remove the whole animal. Clean thoroughly with antiseptic.*

Natural remedies

If you haven't any first aid supplies with you in the wilderness, don't panic: it does not mean you can't do anything to help yourself or others. There are some common ailments that can be treated in a wilderness survival situation using the plants and wildlife you may find around you. There are many plant remedies that can take care of ailments that are widespread over the globe.

MINOR CUTS
By far the most widespread plant of this kind, with many uses, is plantain. Many people use the crushed leaves to relieve the irritation of insect bites. Historically, however, plantain leaves were chewed into a pulp and used to treat minor cuts. Plantain tea is also very helpful for soothing a cough. It is made by putting approximately 10ml/ 2 tsp of dried leaves in a mug of boiling water and leaving them to infuse for 10 minutes.

COLDS WITH FEVER
Elder is a common shrub, or more rarely a tree, that grows in many areas with temperate climates; it is familiar as the source of elderberry wine, which is said to prevent winter colds. The flowers, fresh or dried, can be made into an infusion, in much the same way as plantain leaves, which will help to cool a fever and alleviate the symptoms of a cold. Elder leaves help to repel biting flies and mosquitoes, and an infusion of the leaves can be dabbed on the skin for this purpose.

DIARRHOEA
Oak bark is traditionally used to alleviate chronic diarrhoea and dysentry (*see page 21*). You need to collect the bark of young twigs in the spring; this can be dried and stored. For the treatment of diarrhoea it can be made into a decoction by putting about 10ml/2 tsp of dried oak bark in 0.5 litre/1 pint of water and boiling it for 3–5 minutes before drinking. The liquid has antiseptic and astringent properties, and can also be used on a compress to treat slow-healing wounds, or as a gargle to help with problems such as infected gums or throat.

▲ *Mosses can be used to bandage wounds and control bleeding. Some, such as sphagnum moss, have antiseptic properties.*

▲ *Plantain can be chewed to a pulp and applied to a wound to help the healing process; it also soothes insect bites.*

▲ *Wounds need to be tended to and direct pressure to wounds needs to be applied if there is any bleeding.*

MAKING A NATURAL COUGH MIXTURE

1 Dried plantain can be used to brew a good anti-cough tea. Put a handful of dried plantain leaves in a bowl.

2 Boil some water and pour it over the leaves. Then let the leaves steep in the hot water for about 10 minutes.

3 Remove the plantain leaves from the bowl and the cough mixture is ready for use.

The importance of hygiene

In any kind of survival situation personal hygiene is critical, especially in avoiding the possibility of cross-infection. It is a common misconception that primitive peoples are less clean that we are, when in fact, in many so-called primitive societies, cleanliness and hygiene are as important as they are in Western society.

There are a host of natural alternatives to soap, shampoos, brushes and toothpastes that are used by primitive societies the world over, and knowledge of these can be useful in a survival situation. A little preparation is needed to produce many of these items, so they may not be a priority for you. In a long-term situation, however, it is well worth spending some time and effort making toiletries.

TOILET PAPER
"What can I use instead of toilet paper?" is probably the question most frequently asked regarding hygiene. There are many things in nature that can be used for this purpose. In fact, anything you can find around you will work when you really need it. A good solution is a combination of dried and wet moss. Use the wet moss first to clean yourself and then use the dried moss to dry off. Some people prefer it the other way around, which, they say, works in a refreshing way.

When there is not a lot of moss around, or in an emergency, you can pick some large leaves from nearby plants. Again, use fresh green leaves first, followed by some barely dead leaves. You should always make sure the

leaves you choose are not poisonous or irritating to the skin. Some people use the inner bark from trees, but getting it entails quite a lot of work.

DEALING WITH HUMAN WASTE
Whatever method you prefer for dealing with waste, observe the following basic rules:
• Always make sure you dig your toilet facility at least 25m/27yd away from your fresh water source, so that there is no chance of contamination.
• Dig the hole to a minimum depth of 45cm/18in.
• Always cover your waste with soil immediately, and when your pit is full, or if it starts to smell even after a layer of soil has been added, fill in the rest of the pit and make another one.

▼ *A good example of a discreet latrine, sited well away from the living area.*

▼ *Make sure your toilet hole is deep so that waste will not be detected by animals.*

▼ *Wash your hands to help prevent unhealthy bacteria entering your body.*

DIGGING A LATRINE

1 If you are staying in an area for a while, dig a latrine at least 25m/27yd away from your fresh water source, to a minimum depth of 45cm/18in.

2 You can make the latrine more comfortable by placing a log or two over the pit. Gather mosses and leaves so that "toilet paper" is always at hand.

3 Each time you use the latrine, add a layer of soil to keep smells at bay. Adding some charcoal from the fire will also help to mask any smells.

▲ *In a survival situation you must stay well hydrated. Food is important in the long term, but is not needed as much as fluids.*

• When using paper, always burn the paper afterwards. Paper can lie around for many years to come and will spoil the environment quickly.

• Make sure none of the items you keep in your pockets can accidentally fall in. Having to fish your knife out of your latrine is very unpleasant.

• As always, wash your hands and wrists when you have finished.

DIAPERS AND MENSTRUAL CARE

Most native peoples use dried moss for feminine hygiene, but very soft, well tanned animal hides have also been used for this and for babies' diapers. Some native peoples make pads from cloth filled with absorbent material such as moss or bulrush (cattail) fluff. Hygiene is important because menstruating women may otherwise attract unwelcome attention from bears.

▲ *Never use soaps or shampoos when washing in streams, lakes or rivers, even if they are labelled as biodegradable. Contrary to the manufacturers' claims, these products will not degrade completely and even a small percentage of soap in the water may destroy the environment.*

A NATURAL DIARRHOEA REMEDY

1 A decoction of oak bark is a good remedy for diarrhoea, slow-healing wounds, or throat and gum infection.

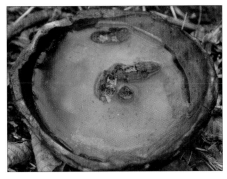

2 Pound the bark and put it in a bowl, then cover it with fresh water, put it on the fire and bring it to the boil.

3 When it has boiled for 3–5 minutes, remove from the fire and allow to cool before drinking like a tea.

MAKING NATURAL SANITARY TOWELS

1 Diapers or absorbent sanitary pads can be made by collecting a supply of dry, springy moss.

2 Put a pile of moss into the middle of a clean piece of cloth or soft, thin buckskin and fold in the edges.

3 This makes an absorbent pad that has many uses. The cloth or buckskin can be washed and re-used.

Making soaps and toiletries

One of the things most often forgotten on trips and outings, but often needed, is soap. It is quite easy to make in the wild and can be a great aid to hygiene, especially in a survival situation.

If you do have biodegradable soaps or shampoos with you, you should be aware that they need soil in order to degrade. So dig a pit at least 25m/27yd away from the water source, to avoid contaminating it, and pour all your washing water into this.

The ingredients you need to make a basic soap are as follows:
• Wood ash or charcoal (which contains alkali).
• Water.
• Oil or fat (either animal or vegetable fat will do).
• Pine resin or needles (these are not essential but will make the soap slightly antibacterial and give it a nice smell).

You will also need some kind of strainer or filter, such as a piece of cloth, to strain the ash out of the water. Always use a stick rather than your hand to stir the ash in the water, since wood ash and water create a very strong alkaline solution that can burn your skin.

Once all the water has boiled off the mixture you will have a good, serviceable soap. You can make it stronger or weaker by changing the percentages of ash, oil and pine resin.

YUCCA-BASED SOAP
Another common way of making soap is by pounding the roots of yucca plants. You get a froth when pounding the plant, which contains a lot of saponin, a lathering substance. The soap that comes from this froth is best used as a shampoo.

TOOTHPASTE
If dogwood or birch are growing in the area, you can chew on one of their fibrous twigs to create a toothbrush. You can use water mixed with wood-ash as toothpaste, but rinse your mouth very well after use to ensure that this doesn't irritate your gums.

A very effective mouth rinse can be made by pounding pine needles in water, then filtering it. The water will smell of pine and be slightly antiseptic.

NAIL AND HAIRCARE
Other aspects of hygiene that are taken for granted are cutting nails and hair. The easiest method of keeping your nails short is to file them regularly on a smooth stone. The stone should have the texture of an emery board. Filing nails may take a long time, but it is preferable to breaking them when they

MAKING A BASIC SOAP

1 First wait until the campfire has cooled down, and collect some charcoal from its centre.

2 Grind down the pieces of charcoal using a stone until you have a fine black powder.

3 Mix the charcoal with water. Stir well, and then strain it through a filter and reserve the water.

4 Heat up some oil or fat and mix the filtered water into it. Bring the mixture back to the boil.

5 Pound a handful of pine needles and add them to the mixture. Boil until all the water has evaporated.

6 Take the mixture off the fire, allow it to cool down and you are left with a good, mildly antiseptic soap.

are too long. Unless you have access to a very sharp, hard stone such as flint or obsidian, it may be easiest just to leave your hair to grow.

If you do have access to obsidian, sharp flakes can even be used for shaving. However, it is important to be extremely careful if you try this, as obsidian can be far sharper than a metal blade and the flakes can cut you easily, since they are not protected as in a modern razor and are often irregular. It may be better not to shave than to run the risk of cutting yourself.

▶ *If you have any small cuts or wounds, you can keep them clean and help them heal by making an oak bark compress. Simply make a decoction of oak bark by boiling it in water, and soak a wad of moss in the liquid when it's cooled down. Secure this over the wound using cordage or a bandage made from cloth or buckskin.*

MAKING AN ANTISEPTIC MOUTHWASH

1 Gather a handful of fresh pine needles and put them in a bowl.

2 Use a clean stone to pound and grind the pine needles

3 Add boiling water, leave to infuse for five minutes, then strain.

MAKING A NATURAL SHAMPOO

1 Dig up a yucca root and trim off the shoots. Scrape off all the soil and cut the root into short sections.

2 Collect a clean rock to use as a mortar and a smaller clean stone to use as a pestle. Then pound the root.

3 Pounding the yucca root produces a lather, which is perfect for use as a shampoo as well as a regular soap.

SHELTER

The first basic requirement of survival is shelter, to protect yourself from the elements. Whether it is to help you survive a single night or for a longer period, a shelter offers you a place in which you can feel safe physically and, just as importantly, psychologically. A good shelter will provide protection against rain, snow, heat and unwelcome wildlife, while allowing you to conserve your body heat and energy and to rest, recuperate and recover. Though the principles of erecting shelters in the wilderness are simple, building one can be hard work. If you try to take shortcuts, your well-being and perhaps your survival may be compromised. If you build your shelter soundly, you will be safe and secure night after night.

Choosing a place to shelter

Finding a place to shelter from the elements should be your first priority in any survival situation. Fire can also give some protection from the elements, but it may be hard to make a fire if you are unequipped. Take the hypothetical example of trekkers in the wilderness who have forgotten this and spend most of the day trying to get a fire going with a bow drill. When they finally realize that their first priority should have been shelter rather than fire, they have spent too much time and energy on trying to make a fire, and no longer have time to build a shelter. They have to spend the night freezing without either a fire or shelter.

SHELTERING NEEDS AND WANTS

If you consider for a moment what you have in a modern house, the list can be overwhelming. Amenities such as flowing water, electricity, toilets and so on make modern life pleasant, but you can survive without them – you don't really *need* them. When thinking about a natural shelter, it is important to distinguish your needs from your wants.

An emergency shelter will normally be small enough to conserve your body heat, and it should be thickly insulated

▼ *If you are travelling across the frozen Arctic tundra, knowing how to build a snow shelter could save your life if you lose your way or there's a sudden snowstorm.*

so heat can't escape and rain can't get in. Conversely, in a hot climate it will need to provide shade from the sun and should be slightly larger with lighter insulation.

When erecting an emergency shelter it is important to preserve energy and time. Ask yourself first, "What are my needs?" The answer is that whatever the environment you find yourself in, you need protection from its extremes. This could mean any of the following:
• cold
• heat
• the sun
• wind
• rain
• dangerous animals

In some circumstances, you may need protection from all of the above. Think about where you site your shelter, and the direction in which it faces, so as to minimize exposure to such extremes.

SHELTER FOR EMOTIONAL SURVIVAL

A shelter can be built entirely with your bare hands, without the need for tools or cordage. A good shelter can keep you alive by conserving your body temperature, so it is not essential to keep a fire alight through the night. Apart from physical safety, it is also emotionally important to have a shelter. It is a place you can call home, where you can sit down to think about your

▲ *If you have no tools, it's possible to make a shelter entirely with your bare hands.*

situation. It is a refuge where you can stay safe in a wild environment. It also gives you a base from where you can venture out to get food, water and fuel.

USING A NATURAL SHELTER

There may be situations where you are forced to find some sort of natural shelter. You may not have time to build anything late in the evening, or you may be ill or weak from hunger.

A natural shelter can be anything in nature that will protect you from the elements. A fallen tree that still has all its leaves and branches can protect you

▼ *The roots of a fallen tree will give some shelter from rain and wind, and can be used to support your own construction.*

from the worst of the wind and rain. Big clumps of vegetation may offer you the opportunity to quickly bend the stems and leaves over yourself. In some environments, you may find caves or natural hollows that can be stuffed with vegetation to insulate them.

If you are stranded in a sandy desert, you might have to bury yourself in the sand to protect your body from the sun during the day. In most situations, however, especially in cold weather, you should try to insulate yourself from the ground in any way you can, as it can quickly sap all your body heat.

It is likely that spending the night in a natural shelter will be the most uncomfortable night you ever spent, but the main objective is to stay alive. You can improve on your shelter, or build a new one, the next day.

FINDING THE RIGHT LOCATION

Consider the points on this checklist when deciding where to build a shelter.

- Ensure that there are plenty of shelter-building materials around you. Dragging them over a long distance can cost hours of unnecessary labour and waste your precious energy.
- Make sure you are close to water, but not in the floodplain of a stream. To avoid contaminating the water, build your shelter at least 30m/33yd away from the bank of a river or stream. This also prevents too much dew from falling on your shelter in the morning.
- Check for any dead branches in overhanging trees, which could fall on your head or damage your shelter. Check for the possibility of an avalanche or rockslide.
- Ensure you are not building your shelter on top of an anthill or other animal shelter.
- Try to find areas that are naturally protected from severe weather, but avoid building deep in the woods. Deep woods take a long time to dry out, and don't get much sun. Try to stay on the leeside, or sheltered side, of woods, mountains and other such protective features in the landscape.
- If you intend to have a fire, ensure you look out for fire hazards such as overhanging boughs, peat-like soil or dry grasses.

WHERE TO FIND A NATURAL SHELTER

▲ *Woodland offers some protection from wind and rain, and there will be plenty of debris to insulate your shelter.*

▲ *Try to make sure there is no heavy dead wood above the site. Remove it and pile it up for firewood, or move to a safer location.*

▲ *Natural caves are always a good option, though you must be careful of other creatures that may have the same idea.*

WHERE TO BUILD A SHELTER

▲ *When looking for a site to build a shelter, try to find a place where there is plenty of raw material within easy reach.*

▲ *Make sure the site is not below a possible landslide. If you have no choice, let the slide happen before you build.*

▲ *You will need access to water, but beware of choosing a low-lying site in case rain upstream causes the water level to rise.*

Building a debris hut

In many wilderness environments, there is plenty of debris such as dead leaves and brushwood available, and a debris hut is the ideal short-term shelter. It is small and well insulated to conserve heat and protect you from the rain. The debris hut is such an effective shelter that it can keep you warm in temperatures well below freezing. It can also be built entirely with your bare hands, so no tools or cordage are needed. The debris doesn't have to be dry, and in a survival situation green material could be used instead.

The debris hut creates a maximum amount of dead air to keep heat in the shelter. It forms a cocoon around you, ensuring that your body is not heating up unnecessary empty space.

AN ADAPTABLE HUT

A debris hut can be adapted to suit the most difficult scenarios as long as you stick to the guidelines shown here. You need to gather as much debris as possible in the shortest amount of time – when your life is on the line, every minute counts. You'll need a thickness of about 1m/3ft around the sides (except the opening) – use a stick to help you judge the amount of debris you've added and pack it down as much as possible.

Fill the interior with the driest, fluffiest material you can find. If there is a lot of fern or bracken around, use

it as a top layer inside the shelter. It smells nice, and does not poke into your body. Make sure you pack it in well. When you bed down in the shelter, you will automatically squeeze the excess debris into the corners and the foot-end, forming a cocoon around your body.

Put some branches over the shelter to stop leaves blowing away. Slabs of bark or a layer of moss will help to stop rain getting through. You will also need to fashion a door by weaving a "bag" from flexible stems and filling it with leaves. You can pull this bag into the entrance behind you to seal it. Trying to seal the entrance with a pile of leaves

▲ *The debris hut takes the form of a dome, which is perfect for shedding water.*

is really cumbersome, and ineffective. Once the bag of leaves is in place, use debris from inside to plug any holes.

Don't worry about cutting off the fresh air supply by plugging the door. There will still be plenty of air flowing in through the leaves. Just make sure you go to the toilet before you crawl in and get snug, as it takes a long time to get in and out of this shelter.

▼ *In order to retain heat, make the entrance of the shelter just big enough to shuffle into backwards, lying flat on your belly.*

▼ *For the framework of the debris hut you will need a strong ridge pole, about 2.5m/8ft long, and two strong Y-sticks, like this one, each about 60cm/2ft long.*

BUILDING A DEBRIS HUT

1 Lie down on the ground and mark out a line around your body, about a hand's width away from you.

2 Dig a pit about 30cm/12in deep in the marked area. If the weather is very cold, try to dig down even more.

3 Create a "floor" over the ground by laying branches along the bottom of the pit, running from head to foot.

4 Create another layer by placing a second row of branches crossways over the first layer. Keep it sturdy and even.

5 Fill up the hole with the driest debris you can find. This layer should be at least 15cm/6in deep.

6 For the frame, plant two Y-sticks at the two corners of the head end, leaning them against each other.

7 Rest a long ridge pole on the Y-sticks, extending to the foot end.

8 Add branches to each side of the frame, lining them up vertically.

9 Fill up both sides of the framework with sticks, then pile debris over them.

10 Pile the debris over the shelter to a depth of about 1m/3ft on all sides, leaving the opening clear.

11 Fill the interior with the driest, fluffiest material you can find. Fern or bracken makes an aromatic top layer.

12 Use pliable green shoots to make a 1m/3ft tunnel for the entrance and cover them thickly in debris.

Building a stacked debris wall

The stacked debris wall is a shelter component that can be used in many different ways. It is simply a double row of poles driven into the ground and woven together with brushwood, with a thick wad of insulating debris between them, so it can be straight or curved, tall or short.

You can use this technique to build a small survival shelter for one person or adapt it to a large construction for a group, perhaps building a number of shelters around a central fire, which will help to retain and reflect heat. It can also be used in other ways – as a hide for hunting, for example. A small semicircular version can be built around the back of a fire as a heat reflector.

THE RAW MATERIALS
To build this kind of wall you'll need plenty of poles. Their length will depend on how high you need the wall to be, but for a shelter they should generally be about 120cm/4ft long.

You'll need a heavy rock to hammer the poles firmly into the ground. You will also need a lot of material to weave the sides, such as semi-flexible brushwood, though in a survival situation you might need to use fresh, green material if there is no dead wood available. You'll also need plenty of debris, which can be of any kind, wet or dry, as long as it creates air pockets.

CONSTRUCTING THE WALL
Having decided on the site for the wall, hammer the first line of poles as deeply as possible into the ground, about 30cm/1ft apart. The second row should be parallel with the first, about 50cm/20in away to allow for plenty of insulation. You might want to put an extra pole at each end of the wall so you can weave around the ends too.

Weave brushwood loosely along the rows to make the sides of the walls. Now all that remains is to pack the space in between with debris.

As a possible variation, you could weave one side of the wall tightly for strength, for example if it is to form the inside of the shelter. If you also weave the outer side tightly you can plaster the wall with "survival cement" (a 50:50 mix of dry grass and sticky mud) or clay. Another option is to build two side walls at each end of the wall, thereby giving you protection from wind blowing in from the side. You could also add a roof using Y-poles to support the front where it's not resting on the wall.

The stacked debris wall is an amazingly strong construction when it is built properly, and a tightly woven wall can last for years. If you ensure that the roof slopes gently you won't even need too much debris to make it more or less waterproof.

▼ *Building a stacked debris wall rather than a complete shelter may save time, but you will need a fire to keep you warm all night.*

BUILDING A STACKED DEBRIS WALL

1 Lay two long branches on the ground or mark two lines indicating where the poles are going to be driven in.

2 Hammer strong, straight poles into the ground 30cm/12in apart, following the first line.

3 When the first row is completed, make a second one parallel with it, about 50cm/20in away.

4 Hammer in a pole between the rows at each end of the wall to stop debris spilling out when you pack the wall.

5 Weave flexible shoots or brushwood between the poles to give the structure stability and hold the debris inside.

6 To neaten the inside of a shelter, or if you intend to plaster the wall, make the weaving really tight.

7 Once all the weaving is completed, fill the whole cavity with debris.

8 Pad the debris down well, checking that there are no large gaps.

9 Plastering the wall with survival cement will help it reflect more heat.

10 To construct a roof over the wall, place Y-sticks in front of the two ends and inside each end of the wall.

11 Place a ridge pole along the top of the wall and a second in front of it; lay sticks across the two ridge poles.

12 Place a good thick layer of debris over the top. A layer 50cm/20in thick should keep out moderate rain.

Building a long-term shelter

All over the world, primitive shelters are built in the round. There are several good reasons for this. When a fire is lit inside (in the centre) the heat can reach everywhere in the shelter, and the walls will reflect all of it right back. In a square shelter, the distribution of heat tends to be uneven, resulting in cold corners. If there are several people in a round shelter, everyone gets an equal share of heat. Round shelters are also stronger than square ones, and they are easier to build.

UPGRADING YOUR SHELTER
Once all the basics of survival are taken care of and you have supplies to last you for a week or more, if you have time and materials available you can consider making your existing shelter more comfortable. Remember though, that you don't want to waste resources

and energy building a shelter that is larger than you need.

To improve on your shelter use the stacked debris wall technique. This

▲ *A long-term shelter can make life a lot more comfortable. Because this can take a long time to build, it is important that all essentials should be taken care of first.*

BUILDING A LONG-TERM SHELTER

1 First make the fireplace. Dig four trenches to carry air to your fire pit and build a hearth with large stones.

2 Cover the trenches with sturdy sticks, so that soil will not fall through and eventually block the tunnels.

3 Pack a layer of soil over the sticks, so that you can walk over the floor without disturbing the oxygen tunnels.

4 Use a line and two sticks, planting the first stick in the central fireplace, to mark out the perimeter of the shelter.

5 Place two markers where the doorway will be. When building the wall, leave this space open.

6 Start the wall by driving 120cm/4ft poles into the ground, following the circle, keeping them 30cm/1ft apart.

means you'll need to collect plenty of poles and weaving material. In this case the roof will be supported by four Y-sticks in the centre, each a good 2m/6ft long. They will need to be very thick and sturdy: the poles shown here are about 12.5cm/5in in diameter. You will also need four sticks to connect the Y-poles in the centre, creating a square. These will also need to be very strong and about 1m/3ft long.

PLANNING THE SHELTER

Think a little about how large you really need your shelter to be. If you are on your own you should go for a diameter of about 3m/10ft: this gives plenty of space for one person and will be easy to heat. Don't overestimate the space you need: a group of six might plan a shelter about 5m/16ft across, but this could accommodate nine.

Before you start building the walls you should construct the fireplace. The fire will burn better if oxygen reaches it from underneath, and you can achieve this by digging four trenches in the floor, one from each direction, from the walls to the centre.

The easiest way to mark the line of the wall is with a line and two sticks. Drive one stick into the centre of the site and tie a cord to this. Measure the required radius and attach the second stick at this point. Now walk around the centre, keeping the line taut and drawing a circle on the ground with the point of the stick.

Next, decide where you want the door. Traditionally, doors face east to catch the morning sun, and this makes sense because it is a mental and physical boost to be woken up by the sun shining through the doorway (assuming you can leave this open). It also allows the sun to dry out any dampness inside the shelter during the morning. If your shelter faces west you may find you wake up a lot later because it seems darker inside.

BUILDING AND FURNISHING

When the poles for the walls have been pounded in you will get a much clearer idea of the size of your shelter. You might even want to build some basic furniture in the shelter now, before the walls and roof are finished, because it is harder to bring materials inside once the shelter is complete.

Consider making a low platform for your bed. Otherwise, if you intend to sleep on the ground, put down a layer of rushes or twigs, then throw about 20cm/8in of debris over this, to keep you well insulated from the ground.

Once you are happy with the interior, you can complete the debris wall by weaving flexible material through the two rows of poles and filling the space between them with debris. You should make sure that the wall is about the same height as your head when you are sitting inside the shelter – about 120cm/4ft – to enable you to sit against it with a straight back.

7 Once the first circle is complete, hammer in the second circle of stakes about 30cm/1ft outside it.

8 Hammer in the four Y-pole roof supports to form a central square; try to orient them on the entrance.

9 Weave brushwood between the poles to create two circular walls with an empty space between them.

10 Fill the area between the woven walls with debris, making sure it is packed in tightly.

11 Use four stout branches to connect the central Y-poles: these must be strong enough to support the roof.

12 Lay sturdy poles from the wall to the central square: these will support a thick layer of debris for the roof.

Before you begin to add the debris, hammer a number of sturdy Y-shaped poles into the ground between the two woven walls. You can connect these with strong branches later on to act as the outer supports for the roof. If you don't do this, the sides of the shelter will gradually sink as the weight of the roof compresses the debris wall.

BUILDING THE ROOF

When the wall is finished, you can connect the four Y-poles in the middle with the four strong branches you selected for this. Make sure that these branches are really sturdy: they should be capable of carrying three times the weight of the roof when you first assemble it. In the lifespan of the shelter, you will be adding more debris as it compresses, and it will also get very wet regularly when it rains. These factors can add a tremendous amount of weight to the roof of your shelter.

Now you can start building the roof by laying thick, sturdy poles from the wall to the Y-pole square in the centre of your shelter. Make sure the poles stick out a little on both the square and the wall. However, you should leave a large enough hole in the centre for smoke from the fire to escape. Depending on how much wind is

FIRE HAZARD

A note of warning. A shelter built of debris is basically one giant bundle of tinder. Take great care to keep your fire under control and watch that embers don't suddenly burst into flame. Even if you come out of it unharmed, if your shelter burns down hours of hard labour will have been wasted.

likely to reach your shelter, your smoke hole should be around 20–30cm/8–12in wide at least.

At the doorway, lay some extra sturdy poles at each side of the door, then lay a very thick branch across the entrance so you can put roof poles there too. When you cannot fit any more poles on to the square of branches in the centre, fill up any remaining gaps in the roof with smaller sticks and branches, until all the major holes are covered.

DEBRIS FOR THE ROOF

All you have to do now is add a thick layer of debris to the roof. Depending on the angle of your roof and the size of the material you are using for this, you may have to weave a layer of supple twigs through the poles to stop debris from sliding down the roof.

A good 60cm/2ft layer of debris on top of the poles and twigs will be needed to stop the rain soaking through into the shelter. Ensure the debris goes all the way from the smoke hole across the whole width of the wall (this is why the roof poles should overhang the wall).

If you find the roof is too high for you to reach the centre in order to pile on the debris, you can leave out the poles at the entrance temporarily, to

▲ *Once all the roof poles are laid, you can finish the roof by placing a thick layer of debris on top, leaving the smoke hole open.*

enable you to throw the material on to those difficult spots from there. Once the roof is completely covered with debris, smooth it out and add some heavier branches to stop the material from blowing away in the wind.

FINISHING OFF THE SHELTER

There are a few things you can do with a primitive shelter to make it more comfortable. Obviously all the building materials you've gathered will be full of small creatures, so one of the most important tricks is smoking out your shelter before you move in, to get rid of all the insects that are now inside it.

You can create a lot of smoke by placing a few embers in a fireproof container and then throwing on some damp, green materials that will produce a thick, pungent smoke. Try using fresh pine needles or sage if they are growing in the area. When the container is smoking furiously, place it inside the shelter for about half an hour. Keep the entrance closed so all the smoke goes through the debris.

Once you are living in your shelter you will want any smoke from your fire to escape through the central smoke hole. You can help to direct it out of the hole by weaving a little square "lid" the same size as your smoke hole. Place this upright next to the smoke hole, facing into the wind. The contraption will act like a funnel, allowing the smoke to escape from your shelter before it's caught by the wind, and stopping the wind blowing smoke back into the hole.

The smoke-hole cover can be made in many different ways. The easiest is to use an animal skin, if you have one, stretching it over a square framework of flexible branches woven together. Keep in mind that the hide will shrink as it dries and expand when it gets wet.

In heavy rain, the cover can be used to close the smoke hole, though you will not be able to have a fire inside the shelter if you do this, as the smoke will have no way out.

▲ *If you are carrying cordage and a tarpaulin, you can rig up a hammock between two trees. This way you can sleep off the ground, which will help you to keep warmer overnight if you haven't got the time to build a proper shelter. Once you've built your shelter, a hammock provides a comfortable alternative on warm, dry nights.*

SMOKING OUT INSECTS AND BUGS

1 Put a few burning embers in a fireproof container.

2 Add a handful of fresh spruce needles or sage to encourage smoking.

3 Put the container in the hut and seal the entrance for about 30 minutes.

MAKING A SMOKE-HOLE COVER

1 Cut some flexible branches to the size of the opening you need to cover. Plant a row of them in the ground about 7.5cm/3in apart.

2 Weave more flexible branches from side to side to construct a sturdy frame. You can make it stronger by tying the corners with some cordage.

3 Finish the cover by tying an animal skin or some large leaves over the frame. In this case, a rabbit skin was just the right size for the smoke hole.

Snow shelters

In winter conditions snow can be used to build an emergency shelter. It has long been used to build shelters by the military of northern countries. The Swedish army, for instance, has built large snow shelters for vehicles and also for use as field hospitals.

When you are trekking in this kind of climate, having the skill to build a proper snow shelter can save your life in the event of a snowstorm. If you lose your way or your equipment fails – for example if your skidoo gets broken – building a snow shelter enables you to protect yourself from the cold.

▼ *In Antarctica this perfect four-person shelter was built from a hundred blocks hewn with the most valuable tool – a saw.*

Protection from the wind is most important, since a high windchill factor can create dangerously cold conditions that quickly lead to death.

When selecting a site for a shelter in a snow-covered environment, keep in mind that the easiest way to build a shelter is by digging into the snow rather than building it up in walls. Look out for places where snow has drifted, or dig around trees and other natural "funnels" where the snow has concentrated and is at its deepest. Of course, there may be situations when you are forced to build rather than dig to create a shelter.

There are three main types of snow shelters, each suited to particular kinds of snow: the igloo is designed for hard

snow, the quinze for powdery snow, and the snow cave, or "drift cave", for drifts. While a lot of different designs and variations are possible, there are a few important things to keep in mind in all cases.

PROVIDING AN AIR SUPPLY
You need to ensure you are protected from the cold, and you want to be insulated, but you also have to make sure there is sufficient ventilation to allow fresh air inside your shelter. When the heat from your body warms the shelter the surface of the snow will melt slightly, forming an airtight seal, so you must cut vents and check them regularly to prevent a build-up of carbon dioxide in your shelter.

WINDCHILL								
Wind speed	Air temperature in °F							
in MPH	40	30	20	10	0	–10	–20	–30	–40
Comparable windchill temperature								
0–4	40	30	20	10	0	–10	–20	–30	–40
5	37	27	16	6	–5	–15	–26	–36	–47
10	28	16	4	–9	–21	–33	–46	–58	–70
15	22	9	–5	–18	–36	–45	–58	–72	–85
20	18	4	–10	–25	–39	–53	–67	–82	–96
25	16	0	–15	–29	–44	–59	–74	–88	–104
30	13	–2	–18	–33	–48	–63	–79	–94	–109
35	11	–4	–20	–35	–49	–67	–83	–98	–113
40	10	–6	–21	–37	–53	–69	–85	–100	–116

Little effect on windchill, little danger of frostbite

Increasing danger of frostbite

Great danger of frostbite

▲ *Once an igloo is completed, melting snow inside will make the joints airtight. The entrance should be a tunnel under the wall, allowing cold air to sink and flow away.*

▲ *Wind can make the air feel much colder than the recorded temperature, and as its strength increases the effect is multiplied.*

KEEPING DRY

When you are building a shelter with snow there is a great danger of your clothes getting wet. When the weather is very cold this is unlikely, but at temperatures higher than -15°C/5°F it can be a serious problem. In all temperatures mittens get wet easily. You should also try not to work yourself into too much of a sweat. It is one thing trying to keep warm when you are dry, but quite another to stay warm when wet.

IGLOOS

If you are in the high Arctic, tundra or other open snow-covered terrain where the temperature is below –5°C/23°F, it is relatively easy to dig or cut snow for a shelter, and the low temperature will ensure that the walls of your structure will stay safely in place. If you are stranded on hard-packed snow you can cut blocks and build an igloo. This makes a comfortable, long-term shelter, though you should bear in mind that it will take time to build and you need a saw or knife to cut the blocks.

Start by marking out a circle on a flat area of compacted snow. For a two-person igloo you will need a circle of

about 2.5–2.8m/8–9ft diameter. As you cut the snow blocks, lay them on their long edges in a rising spiral, stepping them slightly so that most of the weight of each block is on the blocks beneath it. When you have completed the dome shape, the inside should be smoothed so that the "steps" inside do not start to drip water as the inside temperature rises. The outer wall should be covered with loose snow to fill all the cracks and make the igloo windproof. It is best to dig a tunnel under the wall for the entrance, but if this is not possible it can be cut straight through the wall and covered with a rucksack or a block of snow.

BUILDING AN IGLOO

1 Cut blocks of hard-packed snow 60 x 40 x 20cm/24 x 16 x 8in and use them to form a circle around the hole you cut them from.

2 Cut away the tops of the first few blocks at an angle to the ground and build up the walls in a spiral. Cut an entrance hole under the wall.

3 Make the blocks lean into the igloo a little more in each row, to create a dome. Trim the last block from inside to fit exactly into the central hole.

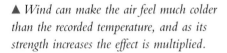

Building a quinze shelter

The quinze shelter looks a little like the better-known igloo, but it is constructed in a different way and is suitable for areas of powdery snow. Obviously when snow is in this condition it has no structural strength and it would be impossible to cut the kind of blocks you would need to build an igloo.

The quinze is made by collecting snow into a pile, which is then left to harden by recrystallizing before the structure is hollowed out from the inside. Making a snow pile of a usable size takes about an hour. You then need to wait for about another hour if the temperature is at least −10°C/14°F. At higher temperatures up to two hours will be needed.

PLANNING THE QUINZE
For a two-person quinze the snow pile should be about 1.8m/6ft high, 2.5m/8ft wide and 3m/10ft long. If you need to accommodate more people, add another 80cm/2ft 6in per person.

Unless time is short because night is falling, the work of piling the snow should be done quite slowly to avoid the diggers getting overheated and sweating. A shovel is ideal for the purpose, but in an emergency situation snowshoes, a billy can or a frying pan can be used to scoop up the snow.

Before you start to make the pile, mark out the area of the shelter and tread the floor to compact the snow.

▲ *If the snow is loose, as it is in northern forests, taiga, boreal forest and coniferous forests, and the temperature is below −5°C/23°F, you can build a quinze.*

CREATING THE SHELTER
On to this floor, arrange rucksacks and any spare gear, bushes and any other bulky material you can find, forming a compact heap. This will help to create the basic dome shape, and will reduce the amount of snow you need to shovel on to the pile. The gear can be removed later. Cover the heap with a layer of snow at least 1m/3ft thick and leave it to harden.

Once the snow has recrystallized, your gear and any other material you have used can be dug out again from the side. You can then enlarge the shelter by digging out from the inside, but you must be very careful that you don't dig away too much and weaken

◀ *Very cold conditions present the dangers of frostbite and hypothermia. If you feel cold, do not fall asleep at any cost. Try to stay warm by moving around, sing songs and keep busy attending to your equipment.*

USING A QUINZE

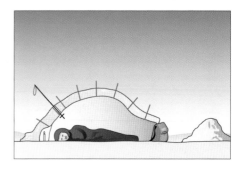

1 The temperature inside should be below freezing, so the snow is dry. Do not make a fire inside a quinze.

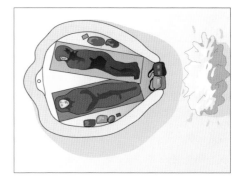

2 Make a small shelf for a candle in the wall near your head. As long as the candle burns there is enough oxygen in the quinze.

the walls. To avoid this, find some sticks and trim them all to the same length – at least 30cm/12in. Poke them at regular intervals into the outside of the snow pile. When you come to dig away the snow from the inside, you will hit the ends of the sticks and know that it is time to stop digging. When the main shelter is complete, you can add a tunnel, digging a trench where

the entrance tunnel is going to be so that the cold air sinks below the level at which you are sitting or lying. It is important to make the entrance just large enough to crawl through. You can use the snow you have dug out of the shelter to create a windbreak outside the entrance. The door should be plugged with snow or a rucksack before you go to sleep.

VENTILATION
The snow walls will be airtight, so you must cut a hole in the roof for ventilation to avoid the possibility of carbon dioxide poisoning. Keeping a candle burning inside the quinze will tell you that there is enough oxygen. The best place for the candle is a small niche in the wall at the end of the shelter, near the sleepers' heads.

BUILDING A QUINZE SHELTER

1 Work out the rough dimensions by lying down and drawing a circle around the users (this is a three-person quinze).

2 Tread down the floor to compact it, then make a pile of powdery snow at least 3m/10ft wide and 1.8m/6ft high.

3 When the pile is complete, tap down the surface with the flat of the shovel to compact the snow.

4 Wait an hour for the snow pile to recrystallize so that it is hard enough for you to begin hollowing it out.

5 Meanwhile, cut some 30cm/1ft long sticks and poke them into the snow to an equal depth all around the pile.

6 When the snow is hard enough, cut out a small doorway. Pile up the snow on the windward side of the hole.

7 Hollow out the shelter, bringing the snow out through the door. When you meet the ends of the sticks, stop digging – the wall is 30cm/12in thick.

8 The roof should be dome-shaped. Make a 10cm/4in diameter ventilation hole in the roof to avoid the danger of carbon dioxide poisoning.

9 Close the doorway using snow or a rucksack, or a plastic bag filled with snow or clothes. You can also make a little shelf for a candle in the wall.

Snow caves and other shelters

If weather conditions worsen suddenly or the light is failing, there may be very little time available to build a snow shelter. In these situations look for natural hollows, perhaps with overhanging trees, that will offer some protection from the wind, or a large drift into which you can dig to make a cave. Tools for cutting snow and ice are an essential part of your survival equipment when you are travelling in arctic terrain, but in an emergency other items, such as skis or cooking pots, can be used to dig a trench or cave. Keep things simple – smaller shelters tend to retain their warmth longer and take less time to build

SNOW TRENCH

The simplest one-person snow survival shelter is the snow trench, also known as a "snow grave". Its main purpose is to keep out the wind. At its most basic, it involves digging a slit trench in the snow with whatever tools are available, adding a roof and then covering it with an insulating layer of snow.

Having dug the hole, dig down another 60cm/2ft at one end. When you make the roof from branches and snow, site the entrance opening above the deeper part of the pit. Lay branches and other material on the higher part of the shelter to form an insulated seat.

If the bottom of your pit reaches the ground, you can light a fire here, but if the snow is very deep this won't be possible. Even without a fire, the cold air will sink down into the deeper part of the shelter, leaving the higher part, warmed by your body, slightly warmer.

▲ *In coniferous forest there is plenty to build an improvised shelter with. A lean-to of spruce branches, with a fire in front of it, makes a good shelter. Make sure that there are logs or foliage insulating you from the ground, and that your fire doesn't melt snow on overhanging branches.*

BUILDING A SNOW TRENCH

▲ *For a quick survival refuge, dig a trench about 1m/3ft deep and wide and 2m/6ft 6in long. This one has a roof made of packed snow blocks.*

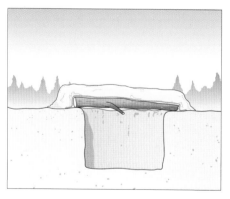

▲ *If wood is available, lay some branches over the trench, leaving one end open, and cover the roof with 30–60cm/1–2ft of snow.*

▲ *By adding brushwood to the sides and piling up the snow you dig out on either side, you can make an insulated shelter in which you can sit.*

▲ *When trekking in arctic conditions, it's vital to carry an emergency survival kit containing a snow saw, ice axe and shovel.*

SNOW CAVES

A snow cave requires a depth of snow of at least 2m/6ft. While the simplest of trenches can be built in under half an hour, a snow cave takes far more time and effort to complete – allow at least three hours to build a basic cave. You'll need digging tools, and because digging will make you perspire, you should remove one of your inner garments before you start digging so that you have something dry to put on when you have completed your shelter.

▲ *Digging your snow cave near the top of a slope means the snow you dig out will naturally fall away from the entrance.*

In a large bank of drifted snow, dig a cave starting about 2.5m/8ft above the bottom of the drift: this saves energy as the shovelled snow simply drops down the hill. You should then tunnel slightly uphill so that your snow cave is higher than the door. In a small drift you may have to hollow out a shallower cave and close up the front with blocks of snow.

As with all shelters, don't forget the ventilation – your survival depends on it. Also, erect a clear marker outside so that potential rescuers can find you.

▲ *If the snow is very deep you can dig directly down and then tunnel sideways under the snow surface.*

▼ *If you are in a group you can dig a number of snow caves in a large drift.*

BUILDING A SNOW CAVE

▲ *Make a temporary shelter in a shallow drift by hollowing out the snow, then closing the entrance with snow blocks and making an airhole.*

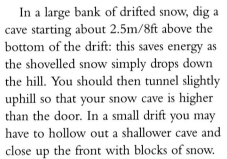

▲ *On a slope, the sleeping area in a drift cave should ideally be higher than the entrance tunnel so that the warmer air stays inside.*

▲ *Despite the flat terrain, the snow here is deep enough to be able to dig down then sideways to make the cave. Ventilation will need to be added.*

Finding shelter in the desert

Deserts pose their own unique problems. Most of these are due to the immense heat present in many deserts during the day. This leads to a lack of vegetation, so that there are few materials to work with when you need to build a shelter. So what do you do when there are no resources in the area around you? What if there is nowhere to dig, nowhere to find wood or scrub, no water and no food? The answer sounds very stark, but it is very simple. If you cannot get to an area where there are resources, you will die.

Deserts actually force you to deal with two extremes: apart from the searing heat of the day, the second is the intense cold of the night, when the temperature can fall very rapidly.

DAYTIME SHELTER

During the day, your main concern will be shade. If you have the materials to hand, a roof or canopy will help you to keep cool. The story is rather different at night, when you need insulation. Most of the time in the desert, however, you'll be travelling

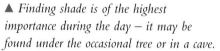

▼ *A desert rock face makes a natural windbreak and radiates heat at night.*

through the night. This means that you will only need shelter during the day, to protect you from the sun while you sleep. In many situations, it is not necessary to build anything.

Shade can often be found under trees or, if there are no trees in the area, you may be able to find caves to hole up in. Just remember that animals

▲ *Finding shade is of the highest importance during the day – it may be found under the occasional tree or in a cave.*

need the same things you do, and may also be sheltering in these nice cool spots. Always check for scorpions, snakes and the like. When you rest in the shade of trees or shallow caves, keep in mind that the sun moves through the day, so be careful about falling asleep in a shady area that may not be so shady any more in an hour's time. It's easy to get burned while you are asleep. As a last resort during the day, you can dig yourself in under the sand, which may be slightly cooler.

SITES TO AVOID

Take great care in choosing a safe site for your shelter. In many desert areas, flash floods can occur during the rainy season, because the rain falls so heavily that the hard, dry ground does not have time to absorb it all. The water will then just run off the surface and collect in rivers.

These floods can become very large in no time, appearing with little or no warning, often as a result of rain falling far away. Sometimes you will find a

▲ *A shallow cave may provide just enough shelter from the sun. Keep in mind that the shade in such a cave may not last all day.*

▼ *A heat-stress index combines the effects of high temperature and humidity to show how much stress your body might be under.*

river where five minutes before there was only cracked earth. These "temporary" rivers can have amazingly strong currents, so it is a good idea to stay away from areas that resemble river beds, the bottoms of canyons, places right at the foot of cliffs and other low-lying areas. It is also important to keep away from areas where rock falls and landslides may occur, as these can be quite common.

USE THE NIGHT-TIME

Heat and lack of water can wear you down very quickly, so you should try to travel at night and rest in the shade during the day. This way you will at least avoid exercising in extreme heat, which will only worsen your physical condition further. Unless it is absolutely necessary, it is advisable even to build your shelter and find your firewood during the night, or at least in the evening and early morning, while it is relatively cool. If in doubt, have a look at what the local animals are doing: where do they find shelter, when do they use their shelter, when do they come out to feed, and where do they find water?

The table below explains the stress placed upon the body in different types of heat. The higher the number, the more stress your body is under and the more dangerous your position is. For instance, if the temperature is 40°C/105°F and the humidity is 50 per cent this means that your body has a stress factor of 135, which is very high. This number is located in the "Extreme danger" zone, meaning that heatstroke is very likely if you continue to be exposed to the heat. Exercise in such conditions heightens the risk.

HEAT-STRESS INDEX

Temp in degrees F	Relative humidity														Heat-stress index
	10%	20%	30%	35%	40%	45%	50%	55%	60%	65%	70%	75%	80%	90%	
70	65	66	67	67	68	68	69	69	70	70	70	70	71	71	
75	70	72	73	73	74	74	75	75	76	76	77	77	78	79	I Caution 80-89°F
80	75	77	78	79	79	80	81	81	82	83	85	86	86	88	
85	80	82	84	85	86	87	88	89	90	91	93	95	97	102	II Extreme 90-104°F
90	85	87	90	91	93	95	96	98	100	102	106	109	113	122	III Danger 105-129°F
95	90	93	96	98	101	104	107	110	114	119	124	130	136	•	
100	95	99	104	107	110	115	120	126	132	138	144	•	•	•	
105	100	105	113	118	123	129	135	142	149	•	•	•	•	•	
110	105	112	123	130	137	143	150	•	•	•	•	•	•	•	IV Extreme danger greater than 130°F
115	111	120	135	143	151	•	•	•	•	•	•	•	•	•	
120	116	130	148	•	•	•	•	•	•	•	•	•	•	•	
125	123	141	•	•	•	•	•	•	•	•	•	•	•	•	
130	131	•	•	•	•	•	•	•	•	•	•	•	•	•	
135	•	•	•	•	•	•	•	•	•	•	•	•	•	•	
140	•	•	•	•	•	•	•	•	•	•	•	•	•	•	

• Beyond the capacity of the atmosphere to hold water

I Caution 80-89°F	**Effect**: fatigue possible with prolonged exposure and/or physical activity
II Extreme 90-104°F	**Effect**: heat cramps and heat exhaustion possible with prolonged exposure and/or physical activity
III Danger 105-129°F	**Effect**: heat exhaustion, heat cramps likely; heatstroke possible with prolonged exposure and/or physical activity
IV Extreme danger greater than 130°F	**Effect**: heatstroke highly likely with continued exposure

Building a desert shelter

When you need a shelter in the desert and a suitable natural feature such as a cave is not available, you will have to build something.

Remember that "small is beautiful" and avoid spending energy on any unnecessary space even if you feel you really want it. Try to make sure the shelter can be well sealed, whether you are occupying it or not, as dangerous animals may try to spend the day there too, especially if you build an underground shelter. This means trying to create a door that fits the entrance snugly, and making sure there are no exposed openings.

USING HOT ROCKS

The most basic method of surviving the cold hours is to find a slope facing the sun, with plenty of rocks lying about. Pick up the hottest rocks you can find, and build some sort of wall around the site where you are going to spend the night. To get most benefit during the night, you should build the wall in such a way that the side of the rock that has been baking in the sun faces you when the wall is complete. The rocks will radiate their heat for much of the night.

If you are in a sandy area, you can dig down into the sand slightly and build the rock wall inside the hollow. Such a shelter could see you through the night. However, it would have to be broken down in the morning and built again in the evening to make it work a second night. You can use the same technique, however, as a natural central heating system in a more permanent shelter.

PIT SHELTERS

In an area of sand or soil you can construct an underground pit shelter. It needs to be about 1m/3ft deep, but don't make it larger than you need: you should just have space to lie down.

You may have to support the sides of your shelter by building walls inside the pit, so you will need to find branches or rocks. You will also need two sturdy beams at the sides of the pit to support the roof. There will be a considerable amount of weight on top of the roof, and you need to make sure your shelter won't cave in during the night.

Use clothing, shrubs or flat rocks to fill all the gaps between the sticks, before adding a deep layer of sand. The main problem with this shelter is fashioning a door to prevent heat escaping and animals coming in.

BUILDING A ROCK WALL SHELTER

1 When building a rock wall shelter to keep you warm overnight, find a south-facing slope.

2 A shallow cave like this is ideal. As it is south-facing, the walls of the cave will retain the heat of the sun.

3 Use any rocks you find strewn about on the slope, which will have been baking in the sun for most of the day.

4 Build a wall using these rocks, leaving just enough space for you to lie. Make sure the hot side of each rock is facing into the shelter.

5 Try to enclose the entire hollow apart from an entrance, which can be located either at the foot or the head end of the shelter.

6 It is important to make this shelter as small as possible, so that your body nearly touches the hot rocks and there is less space to heat.

BUILDING A SAND PIT SHELTER

1 You need to be in an area where there is sand or soil that you can dig and some wood or shrub.

2 Mark out an area for the pit, which should not be more than 30cm/1ft longer and wider than your body.

3 Start digging the pit, using any tools you have or your bare hands. It will need to be about 1m/3ft deep.

4 If the soil is sandy, you may have to build retaining walls inside the pit to prevent the sides collapsing.

5 Even if the soil is not sandy, you will need to lay two beams alongside your pit for the roof to rest on.

6 Gather some strong branches and lay them across the pit to begin constructing the roof.

7 Leaving an opening near the head-end, pile flat rocks on the sticks.

8 Cover the rocks with sand or soil to form the ceiling.

9 Try to eradicate all the gaps, so sand can't fall through into the pit.

10 Place a good layer of sand over the rocks as insulation. Form a slight dome over the area, so any water can run off.

11 Make sure you leave an opening that runs the entire width of the shelter and is large enough to squeeze through.

12 The shelter needs to be easy to spot, both for yourself when out roaming, and for potential rescuers.

Building a jungle shelter

In the jungle, the main concern is often rain. The shelter you will make has to withstand the rain, offering you a well-protected, dry spot inside. Palms are usually very abundant in rainforests, making their leaves the ideal material for your shelter. Bamboo is another natural tropical material you can adapt to build a workable shelter. The shelter shown here uses cohune palm leaves.

MAKING THE LEAN-TO FRAME
You will need six poles, each about 2–3m/6–10ft long, to make the frame on which the roof will rest. Drive two poles into the ground about 2–3m/6–10ft apart. Another pole is then tied to the top of these uprights. You can use any kind of vine as cordage to tie the frame together; the bark of various

▲ *A woven palm-leaf structure makes an ideal roof and walls. The shelter will be more comfortable if you raise the floor surface to avoid the jungle damp and the myriad insects.*

COVERING A ROOF WITH PALM LEAVES

1 Locate a suitable palm tree. The cohune palm has large divided leaves that can be arranged like thatch to channel water off the roof.

2 Use a machete to chop down the stems of the palm and trim the fresh leaves. You will need enough leaves to set closely together on the frame.

3 Split each palm leaf in two all the way down its length, starting from the tip. If you try to split it from the thick end it may break.

4 The next stage is to collect enough vines to use as cordage. This will then be used to tie the frame together and to tie on the leaves.

5 Starting from the bottom of the frame, lay the halved leaves crossways with the fronds hanging down, and alternate the direction of the leaves.

6 The last palm leaf to go on the frame should be unspliced. This will provide an "eave" to channel the raindrops away from the front of the shelter.

forest species is also suitable. The three remaining poles are arranged at an angle from the ground to the crossbar to form a lean-to frame.

WEAVING THE PALM LEAF ROOF
Cut down some palm leaves from a tree (you'll need quite a few) then splice the palm leaves in half: this is easy to do by splitting the tip of the stem and working your way down. Splice most of the leaves before you start attaching them to the frame.

The split palm leaves are laid on top of the wooden frame, starting at the bottom. Arrange them so that the

▲ *Tropical rainforest provides an abundance of raw materials with which to build shelters. The main challenge is keeping dry.*

fronds hang down, directing the water to the back of the roof. Use alternate sides of the leaf each time to create a good watertight "cross-hatching". Once a full row of palm has been placed on the frame, tie it to the bars and add the next layer, until you have covered the whole structure. If you wish you can extend the top of the roof a little in front of the uprights when building the frame, to keep the rain off the front of the area.

You can use the same palm leaves to make yourself a comfortable mat to sleep or sit on inside the shelter. Lay them in alternate directions, as before, for maximum comfort.

▲ *A machete, or parang, is a sharp slashing bushcraft tool for the jungle. Look for handles with riveted plate grips and always sheath the blade when not in use.*

▲ *Bamboo is one of the jungle's most versatile plants. It is a rich source of food and its exceptionally strong wood is used to construct everything from chairs to bridges.*

BUILDING A TROPICAL A-FRAME SHELTER

1 Lash two branches or bamboo poles together to make an A-frame and erect it against a tree for support. Set up a second A-frame about 2.5m/8ft away.

2 Secure a long branch in the V-shaped tops of the A-frames. Tie two poles to the sides and lash a groundsheet around them to make a raised bed.

3 Spread a tarpaulin over the top of the frame to protect the bed from the rain, and keep the roof taut by tying the corners to surrounding trees.

FIRE

Creating a fire without recourse to matches or a lighter is one of the most crucial survival skills you can master. Once a fire is built and lit it gives warmth, provides light during the long dark hours of night, enables you to cook food, sterilize water and make tools, and helps to keep your spirits up. Starting a fire using friction is not an easy task, and the various techniques require a lot of skill. Even then, being able to conjure a burning ember by rubbing sticks together is only half the skill. Tinder does not burn for long, so it is equally important to know how to build a fire that lights with the smallest flame and stays lit.

Fire for survival

Of the four basic building blocks of survival, the need for fire may seem least urgent, but you will often need to start a fire even before you can think about water. The reason for this is that even in the most remote places on earth, water may not be safe to drink unless it is purified first. In addition to bacteria, viruses and other natural contaminations, there may also be chemical pollutants in the water. These could have come from a plane dumping its fuel, farmers spraying insecticide on their fields, illegal dumping or the discharge of chemical waste farther up a watercourse. There are many possible ways for water to be contaminated, but many of the risks can be reduced or eliminated by boiling water before you drink it.

Apart from this vital procedure, fire allows you to create containers in which to carry water, and can help you shape tools to take care of your other needs. Fire will help you stay warm and comfortable. It will also ward off potentially dangerous wildlife and generally make the camp feel safer.

▼ *Knowing how to make a fire may be vital to survival, as water is often contaminated and needs to be purified by boiling.*

SITING A FIRE

Before you can even begin trying to make a fire, you have to consider the best location for it. There are a few important rules to remember:
• To make sure the fire starts easily and burns without too much smoke, you need to build it on dry ground. This is not always possible, however, and if the area is wet it is best to create a dry base using bark or large stones. Once the fire has caught and is burning brightly, the dampness or rain should not matter too much.
• If you can find a feature such as a large rock or a small dip in the ground, the natural surroundings will act as a windbreak and help to reflect the heat of the fire. If it is very windy but there are no natural windbreaks or hollows, you will need to site the fire below ground level in a trench, downwind from your shelter.
• As when choosing a site for your shelter, it is always a good idea to build a fire where there is plenty of material to use for fuel. You don't want to have to walk a long distance each time you need more wood for the fire.
• Before lighting a fire you must ensure that there are no flammable materials on the ground, such as dry leaves. In

▲ *Not only is a fire warming, but getting it to light can make you feel you have achieved something important. A fire also creates a sense of increased security.*

extremely dry regions, the roots of trees or accumulated underground debris could easily start smouldering and might eventually start a fire far away from the original site of the camp fire. When there are flammable materials on the ground you should clear an area at least 120cm/4ft across. Try to build the fire at least 2m/6ft 6in away from your shelter to make sure it stays safe: a debris hut can act like a gigantic tinder bundle.
• If the ground is wet or contains flammable materials such as tree roots, and you need to line the fire pit with stones, make sure they are not waterlogged otherwise you could end up having to protect yourself from exploding rocks (*see panel opposite*).
• Do not make the fire any larger than necessary, both to avoid accidents and to conserve fuel. Placing a circle of stones around the edge of the fire helps to define its size.
• Finally, make your fire in a location where you can watch it at all times.

CLEARING UP YOUR FIRE

When you go into the wilderness to practise your survival skills, it is important to leave the natural beauty of the area intact when you depart. This means that when you have finished with your fire you should remove all visible traces of it.

If you want to preserve the embers for the duration of your journey so that you can make a new fire somewhere else, scoop them up and put them into a non-flammable container, such as an old tin can. Make sure the fire is completely extinguished by dousing it with a lot of water, then check whether there is any warmth or smoke still emanating from it. If there is still a trace of heat or smoke, douse it again.

Ideally, all wood should have been burned away before extinguishing the fire, but if this has not been possible, remove and bury any half-burned

SUCCESSFUL SMALL FIRES EVERY TIME

Here are some tips to help you make a small fire that will burn efficiently and keep you warm and comfortable.
- When you dig a pit for the fire, try to give it gently sloping sides. This will help to keep the burning materials gathered in the centre of the fire, making them burn longer and hotter.
- Build a horseshoe-shaped wall on the opposite side of the fire to where you are sitting. You should make this wall as smooth as possible, preferably using stones, to help it reflect the heat back towards you. Keep the wall about 60–90cm/2–3ft away from the fire and about 90cm/3ft high.
- Another wall, or a natural feature you can sit against, will reflect the heat passing you. A grassy bank, a pile of logs or a stump would do fine instead of a solid wall.
- If you are in a larger group of people, you might want to build both walls far enough away from the fire for you all to sit inside them and keep your backs warm.

pieces of wood. Remove the ashes and scatter them around the area. Then remove any stones you used to border the fire, and fill in the pit with the soil you dug out of it. Camouflage the area so it fits in with the landscape, for example by drawing the forest debris back over it. This way, the area will look pristine when another person passes through in the future.

PREPARING A SAFE, EFFICIENT FIRE

1 Locate a suitable piece of ground that is free of debris, or clear the site, then dig a shallow pit about 15–25cm/ 6–10in deep, with sloping sides.

2 Place rocks on the bottom of the pit, to help reflect any heat upwards. You can also line the far side of the pit to reflect the heat towards you.

3 Gather all the resources you need to start your fire and maintain it. In a desert area there may not be much available, but at least it will be dry.

4 Build a simple reflecting wall about 1m/3ft from the fire using rocks, logs or whatever you can forage, to reflect the heat back towards you.

5 A wall behind you will reflect any heat that passes you back in your direction. This is a highly efficent way of channelling the available heat.

EXPLODING ROCKS

Select the rocks you use at the bottom of a pit with care. You should never use stones that may have water trapped inside them, as this can turn to steam when the stones are heated up, leading to an explosion. To avoid this, never collect rocks from stream beds or from the bottom of valleys. It is not necessary to find completely dry stones, so long as they are not waterlogged.

Firelighters and fuels

All over the world people use numerous different fuels – including dried grasses, wood of many different trees and dried animal excrement – to start and maintain fires.

The first rule when gathering fuel is that it must be dry. This sounds obvious, but it may be very hard in some survival situations. It is also a good reason to gather plenty of fuel at the outset. You should have enough to last at least the whole night, as you don't want to have to go out to find more dry fuel in the dark or when it has started to rain.

▶ *Firewood needs to be as dry as possible, though larger pieces will burn even if damp once the fire is well established.*

▲ *Always try to collect dead wood that is still hanging in the trees to burn in your fire, as it will be drier and less smoky. For kindling purposes, the dead twigs in the left hand above are better for starting a fire than the leaves, even though they are dead.*

▲ *Use a flint or sharp stone to lift the bark off dead wood. The dry inner bark can be shredded into loose fibres to use as tinder.*

KINDLING FOR GETTING FIRES STARTED

▲ *Dry grass may burn well, but is not great as a fire starter because it will remain whole after burning, cutting off vital oxygen.*

▲ *Dry seed heads are excellent for catching a spark. They will allow your ember to grow before you place it in the tinder.*

▲ *The high oil content of dry gorse or furze means it catches light easily and burns well when used as kindling.*

▲ *Dry leaves burn brightly but, just like grass, remain intact, often smothering the fire. Never use leaves to light your fire.*

▲ *Dry plant stalks can be shredded to form excellent tinder or can be used as kindling, though they often burn away fast.*

▲ *Dry sticks are the material of choice to build your fire with. If they are thin they also make excellent kindling.*

THE IDEAL WOOD FOR FIRE

If possible, try to gather dead wood exclusively from standing trees, because when it has been lying on the ground for a while it will probably have soaked up moisture, with the result that it will create too much smoke when burned.

Five different grades of fuel are needed to make a fire, from tinder, to catch the first spark, to large logs.

TINDER

In a survival situation in which you need to light a fire by a friction method, and not with a flame from a match or lighter, tinder is the first and most important component. Basically, it is any soft, fluffy, dry material that will ignite from a spark.

You can use any fine, dry plant material, such as fluffy seed heads or the dry inner bark of dead wood. Fibre that you would normally use to make cordage is usually a great source of tinder. The best way to learn what works well is to experiment.

Having collected the material, you need to break it down with your hands into separate plant fibres, teasing and fluffing it up until you have a soft, dry ball about the size of a grapefruit.

KINDLING

Though a larger firelighter than tinder, kindling is still small: you should be looking for twigs about as thick as a pencil. It also has to be totally dry. Just as with tinder, you always need far

▲ *Sticks ranging from thin twigs to boughs as thick as a wrist are generally referred to as small bulkwood. They make up most of the wood that is used in a fire once it is lit.*

more than you think – if you gather three or four times as much as you think you will need, that should be enough. Always bear in mind that if you do not select your tinder and kindling carefully, all your fire-making efforts might come to a frustrating halt.

As an alternative type of firelighter, you can try making a "fuzz-stick" (*see below*). This is a larger stick carved in thin slivers down to the dry wood: the slivers should be left attached like many small "branches" on a tree.

SQUAW WOOD

Named after the Native American women who gathered this wood in large quantities, squaw wood ranges in size from the thickness of a pencil to that of a finger. If you don't mind a lot of smoke, you can use this wood when it is slightly damp.

▲ *Bulkwood is used to keep a fire going. Though it burns for a long time, it needs small bulkwood to keep it going, and may be smoky if the fire isn't hot enough.*

SMALL BULKWOOD

This is the kind of wood you will mainly be burning. The thickness ranges from marker-pen size to the thickness of your wrist. This is the most important size, as the wood is large enough to give off the heat you need, but small enough to burn on its own without failing. You will need to get your fire established using this size of wood before you can get larger pieces of bulkwood to burn.

BULKWOOD

This is the type of fuel that is too big to break. You would want to use it only to make a large fire, or to keep the fire burning overnight. Never waste energy trying to cut wood this size – just let the fire break it for you. This size of wood can be wet if you don't mind the smoke.

MAKING A FUZZ-STICK

1 If you have a blade suitable for carving you can make this firelighting aid. Select a dry stick, preferably of birch or another resinous wood.

2 Carve deep cuts into the stick, layering them like the scales on a fish. Don't cut right through the wood, but leave the slivers hanging on it.

3 By carving these "scales" you are essentially enlarging the surface area of the wood. This means the fire has more wood to "get at" to ignite.

Lighting fires using friction

There are many ways to light a fire besides using matches or a lighter, and they have been around a lot longer than these artifical methods of creating a flame. Learning the so-called "primitive" ways will enable you to light a fire when your matches get wet, run out or if you don't have any.

Ancient peoples all over the world used these methods. Their very lives depended on their skill, and it is still truly awesome to watch somebody learn this age-old skill, seeing that look on their face when they first manage to get an ember after hours of trying. It is always a special feeling when the ember forms itself, even after you have started hundreds of fires.

The friction method (which applies to all of the techniques described in this chapter apart from the Arctic fire) depends on the fact that two pieces of

wood rubbed together at speed will generate enough heat to produce carbonized particles and sparks, which will ignite a ball of dry tinder. The trick lies in not only getting the correct technique but also having the right mindset. You will probably come to understand this when you learn to make fire, and it is also true of other techniques of survival.

THE FIRE PLOUGH

A simple firelighting technique using the friction method that works quite well in some circumstances is the fire plough. As a sharpened stick is rubbed up and down in the groove of a fireboard, small fragments of wood dust collect at the bottom of the groove, and will eventually ignite into an ember when there is enough heat. You must take care not to scatter the dust by an

erratic stroke of the plough. This procedure can be fairly laborious, and the friction techniques described on the following pages are usually preferable if there is an option.

THE DRILL METHOD

The bow drill and hand drill (*see pages 56 and 60 respectively*) are traditional ways of generating enough friction to create a spark. Each technique relies on a stick being spun at speed in the notch of a "hearth-board" to create embers. The Native Americans have a neat way of describing the process: they tell their children that making a fire resembles making a baby. They liken the drill to the male reproductive organ, while the hearth-board is the female. The ember is created in the notch, like the embryo forming in the womb.

MAKING A FIRE PLOUGH

1 Find a strong stick of hard wood and carve the tip to make a sharp edge like that of a screwdriver.

2 Split a thick branch of softer wood or shave off one side to make a flat fireboard about 60cm/2ft long.

3 With a sharp stone carve a groove about 45cm/18in long for the plough to move along.

4 Place the plough in the groove, and start moving it back and forth. At first nothing will seem to happen.

5 After a while, you will notice smoke coming off the fireboard and plough, and the groove will darken.

6 Wood fibres collect at the bottom and with a lot of speed and pressure, they will ignite into an ember.

SOURCES OF WOOD FOR LIGHTING FIRES BY FRICTION

▲ *Alder is a medium-hard wood, often used for carving reasonably efficient drill sets.*

▲ *Cedar bark makes excellent kindling and the wood is good for making bow drills.*

▲ *Poplar can be used to make successful drill sets, and it is also slow-burning.*

▲ *Elder branches have a soft, pithy centre, which works well to help extend an ember.*

▲ *Stout, woody mullein stalks also have a pithy centre and make good hand drills.*

▲ *Burdock is another large herb with rigid, woody stalks that are good for fire-making.*

DRILL-MAKING MATERIALS

You need medium-hard wood to make a drill, and some of the best species for this purpose are shown above. If you're not sure what kind of wood you have, it's quite easy to test its hardness by running your thumbnail down the length of the stick.

Apart from wood, to make a bow drill you will need a length of cord about 60–90cm/2–3ft long, and you can make this by braiding plant or tree fibres. The best fibres come from stinging nettles stems, but many other plants are also suitable. The dry stems need to be pounded with a rounded stone to separate the fibres, which can then be twisted or braided together.

Another solution is to use spruce roots, which also work extremely well. To find spruce roots, simply dig around the base of a spruce tree. When you come across a root, follow it through the ground, carefully extracting it as you go along. The roots are usually quite close to the soil surface and grow straight out from the tree. When you have collected a few roots, rub them over a branch to get rid of the bark. The roots can be quite long and it is better to use them as single lengths, because they are more likely to break if they are tied in knots.

TESTING WOOD FOR HARDNESS

1 Find a dry stick of the material you intend to use for your bow drill. Cut down the stick to expose a flat area.

2 Run your nail from one end of the stick to the other. You do not have to follow the grain.

3 If the line is crumbly the wood is too soft or rotten. If there is no line or it's only barely visible, it's too hard.

The bow drill

The bow drill is the staple means of lighting a fire by friction. It works on the same principle as all other methods, but is the easiest to use. It is efficient and works even in damp conditions.

SELECTING AND CARVING THE WOOD

To make a bow drill set you will need some suitable pieces of wood from which to make the three carved components, a slightly curved stick (which does not have to be flexible) for the bow, and some cordage. You will also need a knife or stone tool for carving. The set consists of several different parts: a spindle, a hearth-board, a handhold and a bow, and for each of these you should select wood that requires a minimum of shaping.

The first component to carve is the spindle, which should be as long as the distance between the tip of your index finger and the tip of your thumb when you hold your hand outstretched. The top of the spindle needs to have a long point, while the bottom should have a shallow point. The spindle should be perfectly round, and the points need to be sharp and even.

The hearth-board, made from the same wood as the spindle, should be of about the same thickness and twice the width. It should be about 30cm/1ft long so that you can hold it steady with your foot, and should have a flat bottom so that it does not wobble.

The handhold can be made of any material as long as it is as hard or harder than the wood from which the spindle is made. The handhold should fit comfortably in your hand, with a thickness at least that of the drill.

The bow is best made with a slight bend, though a completely straight stick will work. It is best to learn to use the drill with a bow about 1m/3ft long. Once you have mastered the technique, you can try longer or shorter bows: even a bow as little as 20cm/8in long may work.

A piece of cordage is attached to the bow and you have to try to get just the right tension when the spindle is twisted into the cord. It should not be so loose that you can pull the spindle up and down while holding it in your hand, but it should not be so tight that you cannot twist the spindle at all: ideally, you should just about manage to twist the drill with effort. The correct tension will also depend on how flexible your bow is, and the cord is bound to need tightening during use, so you will need to make adjustments. For this reason, you should tie a permanent knot at one end, but a semi-permanent knot that is easily undone at the other.

MAKING A BOW DRILL

1 Gather three pieces of wood: the pieces for the hearth-board and the spindle should be about 2.5cm/1in thick. The handhold should be thicker.

2 First carve the spindle: it needs to be straight, perfectly round and smooth, about 2.5cm/1in in diameter and 20–23cm/8–9in long.

3 Carve or abrade (scrape away) one end to a fairly deep point, about 2.5cm/1in long. This point will become the top of the drill.

4 Abrade the other end into a much shallower point, about 6mm/¼in deep. This end will be the bottom.

5 After use, both points may look very similar, so to make sure you remember which is the top, carve a notch.

6 The finished spindle should be straight, with a shorter and a longer point, and a notch around the top.

7 To prepare the hearth-board, carve a small hole a spindle's width from the edge. This is where the bottom end of the spindle will go.

8 Make a similar hole in the handhold, positioning it above the line on the palm of your hand running up from your wrist, clear of your fingertips.

9 Fasten the string to the bow. Use a permanent knot at one end and one that is easily undone at the other, as you may need to tighten it frequently.

10 Twist the spindle into the string, ensuring that the string is between the bow and the spindle (the spindle is on the outside of the bowstring).

11 With your left foot on the hearth-board, wrap your arm around your left leg, and place the spindle in the holes in the hearth-board and the handhold.

12 Start to move the bow back and forth vigorously. The action will drill round impressions in the hearth-board and the handhold.

13 When the whole diameter of the drill has been drilled into the hearth-board, you can stop. By now, there should also be a hole in the handhold.

14 Grease the handhold so the spindle rotates smoothly. The notch will stop you accidentally putting the greased end of the spindle in the hearth-board.

15 Carve or abrade a wedge shaped notch in the hearth-board, nearly, but not quite, reaching the centre of the hole you have drilled.

PREPARING THE BOW DRILL SET

Before you can start making fire you must drill holes to take the spindle in both the hearth-board and the handle. This is done by using the spindle itself to enlarge small guide holes made with the point of your knife or another sharp tool. The drilling action is the same as that used for making fire, and for this you need to practise getting into the right position to make the drill work efficiently.

GETTING INTO POSITION

These instructions are written for a right-handed person – if you are left-handed you will need to reverse them.

Kneel down on your right knee, while placing your left foot over the hearth-board. The arch of your left foot should be right beside the hole where the drill is going to be once it's in place. Your left knee should be bent at a right angle. Now you are ready to twist the spindle into the cord on the bow so that it is outside the string, meaning that the string is between the spindle and the bow.

Rest your chest on your left knee, and wrap your left arm, holding the handle, around the outside of your thigh and across your shin. Your wrist and thumb pad should be pressing against your leg with the handhold facing down. Position the drill with the top in the handhold and the bottom in the hole on the hearth-board.

THE RIGHT STROKE

The spindle should now be standing perfectly upright between the handhold and the hearth-board. If this is not the case, try to adjust the angle of your left knee slightly until the drill is pointing straight down into the hearth-board. Once your angles are nice and straight, grasp the bow with your right hand.

To get the most out of each stroke, grip the bow as far back as you can. Move it slowly backwards and forwards while keeping the bow parallel with the ground. Once you get a feel for the technique and once your strokes are steady and regular, you can try to speed up a bit with the bow.

If your technique is correct – with the right pressure on the handhold, keeping the spindle steady and vertical and the bow horizontal and going at the right speed – you should start to get some smoke and black dust around the edges of the hole in the hearth-board even if you are not going too fast with the bow. Don't worry if you are not getting any smoke at first. It takes a bit of practice to get it right. The usual problem is not holding the drill steadily enough and at the same time not applying enough downward pressure. You should be spending about 25 per cent of your energy holding your wrist tight against your left leg, 50 per cent pushing down and 25 per cent moving the bow back and forth.

Once there is plenty of smoke, you can increase the speed of the bow a

little while applying more downward pressure. You can stop drilling once the whole diameter of the spindle is in the hearth-board.

COMPLETING THE BOW DRILL

At this point, it is time to grease the handhold to reduce the friction there, and to carve a notch to collect the black dust and eventually the ember.

The hole in the handhold can be greased with the oil from crushed pine needles, animal or vegetable fat, the oil from your skin or hair, or anything else you have available. But don't use water – it will not lubricate the top of the spindle and it will make the wood swell, shrinking the hole and thus creating more friction. Once you have greased the top of the spindle, you must never put the greased end into the hole on the hearth-board because you need friction there.

▲ *Use medium-hard woods for your DIY wood-burning kit, such as hazel, cedar, poplar or sycamore, and look for pieces that require minimal shaping.*

The notch in the hearth-board is important as it will collect all the dust created by the friction, and the size of the notch makes a big difference in performance. It should be a perfect eighth of the hole and should stop just short of the centre of the hole. Divide the circular hole into 16 segments and then carve out the two segments closest to the edge of the hearth-board. Make sure the sides of the notch are smooth.

Now your set is ready to create an ember. At this point you should construct your fire and prepare the tinder to receive the spark. The tinder bundle, made from fine, dry fibres, should be fluffy and in the shape of a shallow bird's nest.

USING A BOW DRILL

1 Place a piece of wood, a leaf or a dry flat stone under the notch in the hearth-board, so that any dust that gathers will not fall on damp ground.

2 Place the spindle in the hole, and start moving the bow at a slow but steady speed, increasing the speed and pressure as smoke starts to build.

3 When you are successful, there will be an ember in the dust in the notch. It may not be visible at first, but there will be sustained smoke from the dust.

▶ *The trick of using a bow drill lies in applying enough pressure with your left arm while holding the spindle steady and upright and ensuring the bow is going at the right speed, level with the ground.*

MAKING AN EMBER

Place the hearth-board with the notch on a piece of dry bark or some thick dry leaves to prevent the hot dust from falling on the ground and getting damp or cooling down. This base will also help you later when transferring the ember to your tinder bundle. Some people like to dig a little hole in the ground underneath the notch to hold the tinder, but this can cause the tinder bundle to get squashed or damp.

It doesn't matter too much whether the notch is facing you or away from you. Check the wind direction and make sure there is enough room to hold your foot down on the hearth-board. Taking up the same position you used to drill the holes, start off again with gentle strokes to warm up the hearth-board. Often it will sound squeaky at this point – this means you are going too fast with the bow or applying too little pressure.

Don't put too much pressure on the spindle just yet. Once the set starts to smoke, you can speed up and apply more pressure. Continue until there is a lot of smoke coming from the bottom of your hearth-board and until it seems that smoke is coming from below the dust in the notch. Then carefully lift off the drill and very carefully remove the hearth-board to see if you have an ember. You will tell from the smoke – if it continues to pour from the black dust you have an ember. Sometimes you can also see a red glow at this point. Once you have reached this stage, you can take a breather to allow the ember to grow. You can also help the process by gently wafting a little air towards it with your hand, but be gentle as the ember is only just forming and is very frail.

Once the ember has settled a little and you've had a few seconds rest, carefully pick it up and transfer it to your tinder bundle.

TURNING AN EMBER INTO A FLAME

1 Hold the tinder bundle slightly higher than your face to prevent too much smoke going in your eyes and start blowing on it gently. Once the ember starts to spread into the tinder you can blow a little harder.

2 When the tinder bundle is nearly too hot to hold in your hands, give it all the oxygen you can. The tinder should go up in flames. You don't have a lot of time to place your tinder bundle in the fire before it burns out, but be careful.

3 If you squeeze the bundle too much, you may extinguish the flames. If you are worried that you don't have enough tinder, place the bundle inside the fire as soon as it's glowing well, and blow it into flames there.

The hand drill

Though the technique and materials are different, the hand drill works on the same principle as the bow drill. The hand drill consists of a straight stick, 30cm–1.5m/1–5ft long and as thick as an average pen, and a hearth-board about the same thickness as the drill and twice as wide. This means that the hand drill involves a lot less material and less preparation than the bow drill. The downside is that the hand drill does not work well in damp conditions, whereas the bow drill will work under most circumstances.

Medium-hard woods are needed for the apparatus. The spindle is often made from hollow straight shoots of plants such as elder, mullein or burdock. The hearth-board should be made from woods such as poplar and cedar. This time the spindle is not pointed at the top or bottom. The only preparation it requires is smoothing and the removal of side branches and knots.

MAKING A HAND DRILL

1 To prepare the spindle, select a straight shoot or branch about 1.2cm/¹/₂in thick.

2 Make sure the stick is perfectly smooth by cutting away any side branches, knots and perhaps even bark.

3 Round the bottom of the spindle to stop it creating excess friction at the side of the hole in the hearth-board.

4 Press the tip of the drill into the hearth-board, about 6mm/¹/₄in from the edge, to make a round indentation.

5 Carve out the indentation carefully. The resulting hole should be exactly the same diameter as the drill.

6 Holding the hearth-board with one foot, spin the drill slowly between your hands starting at the top of the spindle.

7 Once you are confident the hole has been burnt deep enough to prevent the spindle slipping, stop.

8 Carve a notch in the hearth-board, cutting a segment of one eighth of the circle, which just enters the hole.

9 If the drill is hollow you may cut the notch all the way to the centre. The hand drill set is now ready for use.

▶ *The hand drill method requires minimal preparation but is a reliable technique only in dry or hot regions.*

CREATING AN EMBER

Place the hearth-board on a stable surface and steady it with your foot, as far away from the hole as possible. If you kneel, as with the bow drill, your left arm should be on the inside of your leg. You may be flexible enough to sit, steadying the board with the side of your foot. This gives more space to move your hands, but it may be harder to apply enough downward pressure.

With the spindle in the hole, hold it at the top between your flat palms. While pressing down, move your hands back and forth across the drill to make it twirl. Work slowly and gently until there is plenty of smoke coming from the bottom of the spindle, then speed up and apply more pressure.

Embers produced with the hand drill are generally frail and burn out quickly.

It may help to have an "extender" to hand to help strengthen and enlarge the ember before you place it in the tinder bundle. This can be any dry, fluffy material that helps the ember grow. Good materials include bulrush (cattail) down, shredded cedar bark or pulverized, dead softwood.

USING A HAND DRILL

1 Place the end of the drill in the hole in the hearth-board. Orient the notch so that it is protected from wind.

2 Start by slowly rubbing the stick back and forth between your hands until you notice the first puff of smoke.

3 Your hands will move down the drill; when you reach the bottom, move up as fast as possible for another run.

4 Try to ensure you use the whole hand, including your fingers, so that there are more revolutions per stroke.

5 Once the notch has filled with dust, and smoke pours from it when you stop drilling, you may have an ember.

6 The ember is generally small and can break very easily or run out of fuel. Try to use it as soon as it's made.

Jungle fire

A method that works extremely well in tropical environments is the fire saw, which is usually made from a piece of dead bamboo, about 60cm/2ft long and with a diameter of 4–5cm/1$\frac{1}{2}$–2in.

The bamboo is split in half and the hearth-board is prepared by laying one piece flat on a stable, dry surface with the convex side facing up. If you are by yourself, you will need to anchor the hearth-board very securely to the surface it's lying on, otherwise get another person to hold it down. Cut a small hole in the convex surface to keep the saw on one spot.

The saw is prepared by carving off any joints in and outside the stick and scraping one of the split sides to smooth it and even it out. This saw is then placed perpendicular to the hearth-board, with the smoothed edge over the hole.

USING THE FIRE SAW

Just as with the other friction methods, you should start slowly, sawing back and forth over the hearth-board until it starts smoking. The pressure and speed should then be increased until there is a lot of smoke or until you can't go on any longer. The ember will form under the hollow of the hearth-board.

This ember tends to be fairly frail, so be careful to extend it with some dry, fluffy, easily flammable material and be sure to handle it gently.

THE FIRE THONG

Instead of the saw, a piece of dry, flexible rattan about 90–120cm/3–4ft long can be used, though then the hearth-board is held upside down, and you saw upwards. This method, known as the fire thong, is very efficient with a little practice.

FIRE PISTON

Conditions in the jungle can often be too wet to light a fire by friction. An ingenious method developed by indigenous people is a device known as a "fire piston". This rapidly compresses air in a small, very smoothly bored cylinder, which makes it very hot. The end of the piston is hollowed out to hold tinder, and the compressed air gets hot enough to ignite it.

The tube itself, closed at one end, is traditionally made of hardwood, bamboo or even horn. The piston can be made of wound thread, fibre or leather, to ensure a proper seal to create the compression successfully.

MAKING A FIRE SAW

1 Split a length of bamboo in half. One half will become the hearth-board and the other half will be the saw.

2 Using a knife or sharp stone, make a little hole in the convex side of one piece of bamboo, just piercing it.

3 Prepare the saw by cleaning up the edge of the other piece of bamboo. It should be rounded, not too sharp.

4 Hold the saw in the hole, keeping it at a slight tilt so as not to saw both sides of the split at once.

5 Move the saw back and forth while applying a lot of pressure. It should start smoking quite rapidly.

6 When the set is smoking profusely, lift the saw. If the smoke persists, there is an ember under the hearth-board.

Arctic fire

By far the most amazing way to light a fire is by using ice. Being able to create an ember using this fire kit is something special indeed, since it is the only natural method that doesn't depend on generating friction between pieces of wood. In fact, no wood is needed at all, apart from the fuel that is to be used in the fire. In polar regions even the fire may be built using different materials – fuels such as dried dung and animal fat are commonly used in such extreme terrain.

To make an ice lens you'll need a block of ice about 10cm/4in thick and about 5cm/2in long and wide. It should be free of cracks and other imperfections that will distort the lens. Carve the block into a round shape, before carefully carving away the edges to create the lens. Don't carve too much material away from the centre,

but make the edges nearly sharp. Once you are approaching the right shape, put your knife or stone tool down, and continue shaping the lens by using body heat to melt the ice where it is not needed. This will prevent you from accidentally breaking the lens. Test the lens by looking through it at a nearby object, and go on shaping until you achieve a clear magnified image.

MAKING AN EMBER

You'll need some very fine tinder to make an ember with the lens. Crushed bark works well, but only if it's fibrous. Hold the lens between the sun and the piece of tinder and move it back and forth until the light is focused on the tinder. This should start smoking very rapidly. By blowing on it gently you should be able to get an ember in about 30 seconds.

FUEL SENSE

There are few materials to use for fuel in arctic regions. You may find some grasses and moss if you are lucky. You may also find some small, stunted trees above the treeline, but they can be few and far between. On sea ice, such fuel may be non-existent. Driftwood or fat will often be all that is available to a survivor.

If you have candles, a single candle gives enough heat to warm an enclosed snow shelter. Remember that excessive heat will melt the insulating layer of snow, get you wet and possibly bury you. You must always provide adequate ventilation, or you could succumb to carbon monoxide poisoning.

MAKING FIRE FROM ICE

1 The ice needs to be about 10cm/4in across and 5cm/2in thick. Carve a circular shape, then pare the edges.

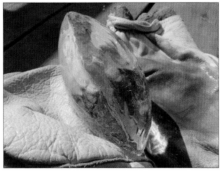

2 The profile of the ice lens shows its shape clearly. The final shaping is best done by rubbing with the fingers.

3 You should strive for a clear, magnified image when shaping the lens: test it by looking through it.

4 When you find the lens's focal point by trial and error, it will quickly char a sheet of paper by focusing sunlight.

5 It is better to hold the lens only with gloves after it has been completed, otherwise it will soon melt away.

6 When the sunlight is focused on a piece of tinder, in this case cedar, it will start to smoke in a matter of seconds.

Building a fire

Having decided where you will site your fire and how you will light it, you need to build it using dry, carefully selected fuel so that it lights easily and burns steadily, otherwise all the effort you put into igniting your tinder will be wasted. Different situations require different sorts of fires. However, the tipi fire is probably one of the best constructions to use in a survival situation. It has several advantages:
• maximum heat
• maximum light
• efficient use of fuel
• smoke and sparks travel straight up
• it is resistant to water and snow.

To build the fire you need a shallow fire-pit, which (in damp or dangerously dry conditions) you should line with dried bark, grasses or stones. Then add the fuel, starting with the smallest type of wood, the kindling. Try to fashion a neat pyramid, but be sure to leave an opening near the ground, because that is where the tinder is going to be put as soon as it's alight.

Aim to put the thinner pieces of kindling nearer to the inside and the bigger pieces to the outside of the fire. Do not pack the wood too tightly at this stage. Leave space for oxygen to reach the centre of the fire, and if there is any wind, line up the opening with the direction it is coming from – it will help drive the flames up into the tipi. If you have any available, it is a good idea to add pieces of resinous bark, such as birch bark, which will combust very, very easily.

Next comes the squaw wood, which is built up in the same manner. At this point, you can also add some pieces of small bulkwood to the fire if you wish. The only problem is that the fire may collapse as the smaller wood burns away from underneath the bulkwood. It is important in any case to feed smaller pieces of wood into the bottom of the fire rather than just piling wood on top. This is especially important if you are using bulkwood, otherwise the fire sometimes hollows out, making it hard to keep alight.

MAKING A TIPI FIRE

1 Dig out a shallow pit with sloping sides to keep the embers in the centre.

2 If the ground is damp or extremely dry, line the pit with bark or stones.

3 To contain the fire, place a ring of large rocks around the side.

4 Break a bunch of kindling in half and arrange it in a pyramid shape.

5 Add slightly larger wood but leave an opening to insert the lighted tinder.

6 You can add a few larger pieces of wood at this point, but not too many.

7 Add the tinder as soon as it is alight, because it doesn't burn for long.

8 Once the fire is lit, you can maintain it by adding larger pieces of wood.

Keeping a fire going

There may be many times when you want to ensure that your fire survives through the night, so you don't have to go through the process of relighting it in the morning. There are various ways to make sure that some embers survive all night, but you must be very sure that there is no danger of the fire spreading and getting out of control while you are asleep.

Once you are pretty much ready to go to sleep for the night, you can prepare the fire to last until the morning by adding some large pieces of green wood. The best wood to use for this would be fresh branches of hardwoods such as oak. However, green wood will cause a lot of smoke, which may be undesirable.

If the fire is sheltered and the smoke will not disturb you, just throwing on a large amount of green wood should make it glow through the night. If the fire is less protected from the wind, you can also throw some soil over the glowing embers once you have placed the green wood on the fire. The soil will prevent too much oxygen from reaching the embers, thereby reducing the speed at which they burn out.

Make sure that the soil does not contain dry leaves, grasses or other such material, because this may flare up unexpectedly.

The next morning, to get the fire going again, all you have to do is carefully remove the soil from the fire. There should be plenty of embers still there, though they may be buried beneath a layer of ash. Use a bit of tinder and plenty of kindling wood to build a small new fire on top of the embers. By blowing at the embers, you should be able to get the fire to light again in a matter of seconds.

DAMPING DOWN A CAMP FIRE

1 While you are getting ready to go to sleep in the evening, leave the fire until it has pretty much burned down. Place a number of thick green sticks on the fire, which will smoulder slowly through the night.

2 Cover the fire with soil, making sure you are not using really wet soil, to reduce the flow of oxygen. In the morning, remove the soil from the fire and carefully scrape the ash away so the embers are exposed.

3 Using some tinder and plenty of kindling, build a small fire over the embers and blow on it to get it going. Once the first flames have started to appear, add more wood, and build your fire up again as usual.

MAKING A MATCH TO CARRY FIRE

1 Collect a good amount of tinder such as bulrush (cattail) down and other small fibres, and find a piece of bark 10cm/4in wide and 30cm/12in long.

2 Roll the tinder into the bark like a cigar. Make sure the tinder is not too tightly rolled, but not too loosely either. A bit of testing is often required.

3 Tie up the bundle with cord and put the ember in the top. The trick is to give it just enough oxygen to let it slowly smoulder down the match.

Building a fire for cooking

A fire for cooking needs to be built in a way that will create plenty of hot embers. When you are roasting meat or cooking food in a vessel such as an earthenware pot, you don't want too many flames. A good bed of hot coals will give a more sustained heat and the temperature will also be more regular, so that your food will cook properly without charring.

Often such a fire is built between two heavy logs, which both contain the fire and provide support for any pots or sticks to rest above the embers. Of course these two logs will burn as well and will eventually have to be replaced. One way round this is to line the inside of the logs with a layer of clay, which will prevent them from burning. The fire will be somewhat hemmed in by the logs, so if there is a prevailing wind, lay them in that direction to ensure a good supply of air.

A tipi fire is initially built between the logs. Once this is lit and burning profusely, thicker squaw wood is added, laying it in the same direction as the two logs. Once these are burning well, more branches are laid crossways and left to burn. The fire will burn down rather quickly, but will leave a lot of embers suitable for cooking on.

From now on, the trick is to keep a good amount of embers in the fire. It helps to add only one stick at a time. This will flare up, but turn into embers

quickly, because there is no additional wood to support the flames. Just keep adding sticks one after the other.

Cooking fires have many other uses. When you light one, be ready to make some glue, strip some spruce roots, or do any other tasks that require a fire without flames. You should light the fire for such activities during the day, as the embers do not provide much light to see by.

HANDLING EQUIPMENT
Apart from some fireproof containers, you also need to make some equipment to get the containers off the fire when the food is ready. Make suitable tools

▲ *The best fire for cooking provides a good bed of embers and should be built with stable supports for bowls and pots.*

before you start cooking, as it can be very frustrating if food or hot water gets lost in the fire because you drop a container or knock it over.

The most useful tool would be a pair of tongs, though separate tools often need to be fashioned for each container you use, since the shapes of cooking pots can vary so much. Try to incorporate features such as handles that sticks can slide through when you are making the pots. For further advice on tools and equipment, see page 108.

COOKING WITHOUT UTENSILS

▲ *Cook fish by laying it out flat on a hot rock, or hang it on a stout log placed next to the fire.*

▲ *Thread meat and vegetables on to straight sticks to make kebabs, then roast them over ash-covered embers so they don't burn.*

▲ *Simple small loaves of unleavened bread are delicious when baked on a flat stone heated by a wood fire.*

CONSTRUCTING A SHALLOW OPEN FIRE FOR COOKING

1 Dig a shallow fire-pit so the embers stay together. Don't make the pit any wider than your cooking pot.

2 Line the pit carefully with either bark or stones. If you use stones, make sure they are collected from a dry area.

3 Place two thick logs on either side of the pit, close enough together to support the pot over the fire.

4 Break a few handfuls of kindling in half and arrange them in the middle of the pit in the shape of a tipi.

5 Leave an opening on one side of the fire so you can place the burning tinder bundle under the wood.

6 Add some slightly larger pieces of wood, again leaving one side open. The fire will now resemble a lean-to.

7 Add small bulkwood if you wish, but take care not to choke the fire.

8 As it is hemmed in, you may need to blow on the fire to get it to light.

9 Once the fire is lit, add squaw wood and small bulkwood to the open side.

10 As the fire takes hold, add larger pieces of wood until a good bed of embers is forming below the fire.

11 Go on adding wood for about half an hour, so that you end up with a good thick layer of embers.

12 After the base of embers is established, keep adding the odd stick, so fresh embers are produced.

Using hot rocks for cooking

As well as cooking your food in or over the fire, you can try an alternative method using rocks, which retain heat well and can be used in various ways. You'll need to gather some large, smooth rocks and place them inside a hot fire that is already well established. Leave them for a few hours, until they are red hot.

CHOOSING THE RIGHT ROCKS
When finding rocks or stones to put in your fire, never collect them from streams, marshes or other waterlogged areas. Always collect them from higher ground where they won't have soaked up a lot of water. When waterlogged rocks are heated, it may be too hard for the expanding water to seep back out, causing the rock to explode. Rocks that appear damp due to rainfall are

usually fine as long as they are collected from a higher elevation. Even then, it's usually a good idea to stay away from them for half an hour when they first go into the fire, just to be safe.

▲ *Tempting though it might be, never remove waterlogged rocks from a stream to use on your fire.*

BOILING WATER
One of the most useful ways of using heated rocks is to boil water. You can use them to heat water stored in containers, such as wooden bowls or animal bladders, that would burn if placed over the fire. A few fist-sized rocks can easily bring several litres of water to the boil. If necessary you can keep it boiling by adding more rocks.

HEATING ROCKS TO BOIL WATER

1 Collect dry rocks and place them in a hot fire. Make sure they are placed right in the hottest part of the fire.

2 Keep adding wood, and use your fire as normal. The stones are ready when they appear to be red hot.

3 Take a rock out of the fire with a pair of improvised tongs and carefully immerse it in water. The water should start bubbling immediately.

4 Add more rocks to boil large amounts of water, or to keep the water boiling. Stirring the water will help to distribute the heat of the rocks evenly.

COOKING ON ROCKS
If you can find large flat rocks, you can heat them in the fire until they are red hot and then use them in much the same way as a griddle or frying pan. This technique is most successful if you have some oil or fat to prevent the food sticking to the stone. It can be used to fry or bake flat bread.

If you have two thin flat rocks you can even cook food such as meat or fish between them. This makes the food taste good as well as speeding up the cooking time.

ROCKS AS HEATING DEVICES
Having cooked your meal, you can also use hot rocks to keep you warm. You can place them inside your shelter to warm up the space, or use them as personal body warmers (though you should make sure they are not too hot).

Cooking food in a covered pit

Another great way of cooking is in a pit, heated with rocks from the fire. You simply put your meal in the pit, let it cook throughout the day, and have a nice meal ready for you when you come back home in the evening. The pit needs to be 30–60cm/1–2ft deep, and the hot rocks are put on the bottom. Wait a little to allow the rocks to dry out the pit, otherwise the food may taste rather earthy.

Once the pit has dried out, put a thick layer (about 20cm/8in) of green grass or large edible leaves over the rocks. Place your food in the pit, cover it with more grass or leaves, and fill the pit with debris and soil. All you have to do is dig your food up again a few hours later. If you put in plenty of rocks, it should be thoroughly cooked. It's worth experimenting with this to see just how many hot rocks you need and how long the food should stay in the pit for the ideal meal.

MAKING A COVERED PIT FOR COOKING

1 Collect plenty of rocks, making sure they are not waterlogged, and place them in the fire to heat up.

2 Dig a pit about 60cm/2ft deep and wide enough to place all the food you want to cook in a single layer.

3 Once the rocks are red hot, place them in the bottom of the pit. The more rocks you have, the better.

4 Leave the rocks for a while so that the pit dries out. Cover the rocks with leaves to stop them burning the food.

5 Wrap the food in large edible leaves and place the wrapped food bundles at the bottom of the pit.

6 The heat from the rocks will rise up to cook the food bundles. Large pieces of meat do not need to be wrapped.

7 Cover the food with more grass and edible leaves. Adding a layer of bark will also help to protect it from debris.

8 Fill up the pit with debris and soil. Mark the pit in some way to remind you where you buried your food.

9 Leave the food to cook for 3–7 hours (depending on its size) then dig it up carefully and enjoy your meal.

WATER

Even in ideal circumstances, human beings can survive for only three to four days without water, and if you are exerting yourself or having to contend with high temperatures, this time will be much shorter. So as soon as your shelter is taken care of, you must make sure you have access to a supply of fresh water. That's easier said than done and if you don't have a modern water filter, then you will need to purify the water by boiling it (this, in turn, makes fire more important in the big scheme of survival). Purification of drinking water could turn out to be your biggest headache in a survival situation. It is essential, however, otherwise you might survive other adverse conditions only to fall prey to waterborne diseases or the chemical pollution that infiltrates many water sources.

The importance of water

About 60–70 per cent of the human body consists of water, and the brain consists of about 85 per cent water. This means that the average person contains about 50–60 litres/11–13 gallons of water. Clearly, water is therefore very important for survival. Every cell in the body depends upon water in order to function properly. We need a supply of water daily, because we cannot maintain reserves of it in our body as we can with food. Numerous disorders are caused by insufficient water, as well as by drinking water containing micro-organisms or polluted by chemical effluent.

In order to maintain the various bodily functions in a temperate climate, the average person should consume about 3.8 litres/$6^1/_2$ pints of water a day. In hot climates, or when working hard, the average person may need to consume over 10 litres/$17^1/_2$ pints of water per day.

WATER LOSS

The table below shows the effects of losing only a moderate amount of water without replenishing it. Looking at this table, it becomes clear that in a temperate climate you would start to feel some unpleasant effects of dehydration after just one day without water. The second row pretty much coincides with the end of a second day without water. This table represents loss of water only in a moderate climate – in extreme situations, the loss of water can be a lot faster.

KEEPING FLUID LOSS DOWN

If you can't acquire water immediately, or if the supply is limited, it is clearly important to try to minimize your loss of fluid so that you need to replace less.

Humans have the capability to sweat away as much as 1.5 litres/$2^1/_2$ pints of fluids per hour when engaged in strenuous exercise in temperate conditions. Couple physical exertion with a hot environment, and you could lose even more. In moderate circumstances, when at rest, the average person sweats about 1 litre/$1^3/_4$ pints per day. This means that by keeping sweating down, you can stop a lot of fluid from being lost from the body.

In a survival situation, you will have no choice but to exert yourself quite

▲ *Natural caches often contain water but it is important to purify it as the water may have been stagnant for a long time.*

regularly to satisfy your daily needs, and this can cause sweating. However, there are a few ways in which you can reduce this loss of fluid.

The first necessity is to master all the skills you need to survive. Spending only 30 seconds to light a fire using a bow drill set, for example, will cost you a lot less effort, and therefore a lot less sweat, than having to spend 30 minutes to get a fire lit. Mastering survival skills also includes learning to be as efficient as possible when gathering the materials you need, again saving on fluid loss through sweating.

THE EFFECTS OF DEHYDRATION		
Loss of water	**Effects**	**Survival chances**
Up to 4 litres/ 7 pints	Thirst, vague discomfort, impatience, nausea and loss of efficiency.	3 days in moderate climate
Up to 8 litres/ 14 pints	Dizziness, headache, breathing difficulty, tingling in the limbs, increased blood concentration, absence of salivation, purplish discoloration of the skin, indistinct speech and inability to walk.	2 days in moderate climate
Up to 15 litres/ 26 pints	Delirium, spasticity, dimming of vision and death.	1 day in moderate climate

SIGNS OF WATER – SIGNS OF LIFE

▲ *Although rivers are often not visible during the dry season, they may still be running below ground. Patches of vegetation can indicate their courses.*

▲ *Often there is water below the ground at the bottom of deep canyons like this one. This may or may not be confirmed by the presence of vegetation.*

▲ *Coarse vegetation is usually found farther away from the underground water source, while the presence of grasses indicates water just below the surface.*

The second way to prevent excessive sweating is to take care of as many of the tasks requiring physical activity as you can during the cool hours of the day. In extremely hot climates, that may even mean working during the night and resting during the day when it's scorchingly hot.

The third method is the simple precaution of avoiding overheating by removing layers of clothing when you get hot. On the other hand, in some climates adding layers can help keep the heat down. A good example is set by various nomadic desert peoples, who are often covered from head to toe in several layers of loose clothing to keep them cool. Covering the head with a turban or other headdress to protect it from the sun is another example.

A lot of moisture is lost through breathing. Again, keeping your core temperature and expenditure of effort down is one way to prevent excessive loss by this means. Another way to minimize loss of moisture is to focus on breathing through the nose, rather than through the mouth. This might seem extreme, but concentrating on small things like this can make all the difference in a survival situation.

Water is also needed to break down food, so when water is short, avoid eating as far as possible. You should also be careful what you drink. Don't consume alcohol, as it will take more water to break down the alcohol than is added by drinking the alcoholic beverage. Coffee is another liquid to avoid when there is little water available, as it has a diuretic effect.

RATIONING YOUR WATER

A common misconception is that you need to ration water when it is short, much as you would ration food. It is important not to do this. The negative result far outweighs the positive result of saving water for later. Sometimes, dehydration can overcome your body too fast to realize something is wrong. A state of unconsciousness can often occur with little warning when you are dehydrated. There are recorded incidents of people having been found dead due to dehydration even though they had a full water bottle at their side. Even when you are short of water, therefore, it is important to continue to drink as normal.

Don't guzzle what you have, however – take it in sips. Be methodical. If you do become dehydrated and then find a source of water, you should replenish your body fluids slowly, otherwise the stomach may go into convulsions, losing even more fluid by vomiting.

CONSERVING WATER

1 When you do have a supply of water, store it out of the sun to avoid excessive loss by evaporation.

2 Suspending a water bag under a tree will keep it cool. Take only as much as you need, to conserve your supply.

Finding a safe water supply

There are many ways to gather water and the ideal source to look for is clear, fresh, running water. Gathering is the first part of the exercise, for which you need manufactured or natural containers. You should then always filter and purify water, but it is a good idea to get it from the cleanest source.

WHAT TO LOOK FOR

Look for relatively fast-flowing rivers and streams, with healthy vegetation on their banks. In stagnant pools of water, it is generally easier for bacteria and viruses to survive and multiply. It is harder for fast-flowing water to sustain much bacterial growth.

One indication of water quality is to see whether many animals come to drink from it or if they favour a different source. This method is not always foolproof, however, as many wild animals build up a certain amount of resistance to waterborne bacteria and viruses that may cause serious illness in humans. The same is true for water sources frequented by the local human population. It is often the case that Western people become ill after drinking water that local people have been drinking all their lives.

If you find what appears to be a good, clean source, check it out as far upstream as you can. It is possible that an animal carcass or some other pollutant may be located just upstream, making the water unsafe.

▲ *Only when you are absolutely certain the water is safe to drink should you drink straight from a stream.*

DANGERS IN DRINKING WATER

Common infections that may be contracted from unclean water include cholera, hepatitis A and giardiasis.

Cholera is the relatively friendly one. It is a bacterial infection that causes mainly diarrhoea, and is treated by continually replacing lost fluid by drinking clean water. (Continuing to drink infected water will make the situation far worse.) Approximately one in 20 of those infected will have severe symptoms characterized by profuse

watery diarrhoea, vomiting and leg cramps. In these people, rapid loss of body fluids often leads to dehydration and shock. Without treatment, death can occur within hours, and such victims may require fluids to be replaced intravenously.

Hepatitis A is rather less friendly; it is a disease of the liver caused by a viral infection. Symptoms do not always occur but may last for up to two months and include fever, tiredness, loss of appetite, nausea, abdominal discomfort, dark urine and jaundice (yellowing of the skin and eyes). Older people are generally more susceptible to the disease than children. Luckily,

▼ *A watering hole on the African savanna may be a hazardous source of water as it will attract many dangerous creatures who come to drink there.*

▼ *Animals drinking water is not always a sign that it is safe for human consumption: many animals are resistant to infections and diseases that can make humans ill.*

▼ *Some wells have a mechanical method of lifting water while others require you to haul it up manually. Never pollute a well by washing yourself or your equipment near it.*

COLLECTING WATER

▲ *One of the commonest ways of collecting water is by cupping your hands and drinking directly from a stream. Do so only if you know the water is absolutely safe.*

▲ *If you have plenty of containers, rainwater can be collected as it falls and does not need to be purified, though it may contain low concentrations of chemicals.*

▲ *If you have a tarpaulin or poncho, set it up on four poles with a weight in the centre to collect rainwater. Keep one edge low to allow the water to run off into a container.*

the disease is not life-threatening, though medication is often required, and once you have recovered, your body will have made antibodies that prevent a recurrence of the disease.

Giardiasis is caused by a one-celled, microscopic parasite that lives in the intestines and is ingested in water contaminated by sewage. Due to its tough outer shell, it can survive outside the body for a long time. Giardia is currently one of the most common waterborne diseases. Infection can

▼ *For a few days after rain has fallen you can often find water in natural hollows in the landscape.*

cause a variety of intestinal symptoms, which include diarrhoea, greasy stools that tend to float, stomach cramps and nausea. These symptoms may lead to weight loss and dehydration. Symptoms may last from two to six weeks or longer, though some people with giardia have no symptoms at all. The disease is generally treated by alleviating the symptoms and allowing the parasite to be flushed out of the body.

ALWAYS PURIFY

If you find a water source where animals appear to drink, where the water flows fast and cold and no dead animals have been found higher up the

stream, you can be reasonably sure the source is fairly clean of bacterial and viral infections. Even then, you should be sure to purify water for drinking, as any infectious agents will not be apparent until it's too late.

CHECKING FOR CHEMICAL POLLUTANTS

Even when the water is free of viral and bacterial contamination, the source may have been polluted by chemicals. The only ways to minimize the danger of drinking chemically contaminated water are to walk all the way upstream, or to check the plant life in and around the water source carefully.

Ask yourself questions such as: "Are there many algae in the water?" (None could be a bad sign, but so can too many, as some algae thrive on phosphates and the like.) Another question might be: "How healthy do the plants growing around the water source look?" Often, when water is chemically contaminated, it affects the health of the flora around the polluted area. "Are there many healthy looking fish living in the stream?" is another question worth asking yourself.

The problem with chemical pollutants is that many will not "boil" away when the water is purified. Filtering through charcoal and the like may filter out some chemicals, but not others. So if in doubt about pollution, try to find an alternative source before relying on your purifying techniques.

Natural sources of water

In most regions, it is fairly easy to obtain enough water to sustain yourself. In a moderate climate there are generally plenty of rivers and streams from which you can take water. However, if you find yourself in an area where there are no watercourses nearby, or where riverbeds have dried up, you need to know how to locate alternative sources.

NATURAL WATER CACHES

After rain has fallen, you may find water that has collected in natural caches such as hollows in rocks. Ideally, you should use this kind of standing water within a few days of the rainfall. A small cache of water that remains for a long period of time can become the perfect breeding ground for bacteria and viruses.

Useful caches of water can often be found in uneven ground. A good example is where rainwater has collected in little holes and hollows in a rocky surface. These sources will often be fairly safe, but even so you should not neglect to treat any water you collect, just in case of some form of pollutant being present.

It is also important to collect as much water as possible from such sources, as the water may be around for only a day or two. Sometimes it may even disappear within hours.

COLLECTING MORNING DEW

Even where no rain falls, changes of temperature at night result in moisture condensing out of the atmosphere and being deposited on the landscape in the form of dew. In the morning you can collect it by wiping it from vegetation and rocks with an absorbent cloth, then wringing it out into a container.

A very successful Australian native method of collecting this kind of water is to tie absorbent materials to your legs and walk through the grass when there is a layer of dew or raindrops clinging to it. It is possible to gather a large amount of water using this method.

▲ *Water may be found in streams such as this, but make sure it is safe to drink by checking for obvious signs of pollution.*

RAINWATER

An excellent source of drinking water, rainwater has the additional advantage that it is free of bacterial and viral infection. It may, however, contain traces of chemical pollution in heavily industrialized regions.

Rainwater can be gathered using the dew collection method, though it may be easier to collect it while it is actually raining if you have plenty of containers to spread over an area.

COLLECTING DEW

1 If you have some spare clothes made out of material such as cotton, they can be used to collect water. Simply tie the material around your feet.

2 Walk through areas of fairly long grass or other plants, allowing the cloth around your ankles to soak up as much dew as possible.

3 Wring the water out of the soaked material into a bowl. Don't forget to purify it, even though dew is not very likely to contain pollutants.

▲ *Birch sap can be tapped from the trunk and drunk as it is, or boiled down to a sweet liquid not unlike maple syrup.*

▲ *Slow-moving streams are often dangerous to drink from as bacteria and viruses can more easily reproduce in sluggish water.*

▲ *Useful liquid can be found in the fruits of many trees, such as the palm. Coconuts have more liquid inside when unripe.*

GETTING WATER FROM PLANTS

In the jungle a common way of getting water is by retrieving it from water vines, which are easily identified by their round stems, 7.5–15cm/3–6in thick. To produce clear water you simply cut off a piece of stem about 1m/1yd long. If the vine produces a cloudy, bitter liquid, you have picked a different species: don't drink that sap. The liquid from a water vine will have a neutral or fruity taste. The downside is that it cannot be stored. Some vines irritate the skin, so gather the liquid in a container rather than putting the stem straight to your mouth.

In Australia, the water tree, desert oak and bloodwood grow roots near the surface that can be prised out of the ground. Remove the bark and suck out the moisture or reduce the root to a pulp and squeeze it over your mouth or a container. Green bamboo thickets are an excellent source of fresh water.

Bend a stalk over, tie it down, and cut off the top. Place a container under the cut, and you can collect quite a lot of water in a few hours.

In deserts, most species of barrel cacti contain water. If you cut off the top you can mash the pulp and suck it dry, though it is not edible. However, unless you have a large tool such as a machete, it is impossible to get through the defensive spines and cut the flesh, and doing so will kill the plant.

PLANTS THAT STORE WATER

▲ *This pitcher plant contains fluid that is drinkable in small doses but beware of insects trapped inside: you need to filter and sterilize the fluid first.*

▲ *Succulent desert plants such as aloes and agaves hoard fluid to help them survive periods of drought. The fleshy leaves can be cut or broken off to obtain the liquid.*

▲ Opuntia microdasys, *a prickly pear cactus also known as "bunny ears", has thousands of barbed spikes that can irritate, but contains moisture in its fleshy pads.*

Filtering and purifying water

Whatever water you get, it is a good idea to purify it. You can never tell for sure where the water has been, and what may be in it.

You should start by filtering the water if it contains debris and larger particles. To do this you will need to make some kind of sieve or strainer. A hollow log stuffed with grass can do a good job of removing larger particles from the water, but if you have a sock you can make a finer filter. The first resort is to fill it with grass, as with the hollow log, but if you have access to sand you can use this to fill the sock filter. Start with the finest sand you can find, and fill the sock with coarser and coarser sand until you reach the top.

Suspend the filled sock over a container, pour in the water you have collected, and leave it to filter through.

BOILING WATER

Filtered water may look clean but it is by no means safe to drink. To purify water, you have to boil it (or use a modern filter or purifying agent if you have access to either of these options).

There are different opinions on how long water should be boiled to get rid of bacteria. It is safer to stick to a time of about 15–20 minutes. This may sound like a long time, but you just cannot afford to risk drinking water that is still contaminated.

PURIFYING AGENTS

Modern methods of purifying water include the use of purifying agents such as household bleach, iodine and water-purifying tablets. Modern commercially available filters purify the water as well as filtering it. The purifying agents are used in the following ways:

Bleach: Add 10 drops of household bleach to 4.5 litres/1 gallon of water and mix it well. Then allow it to stand for 30 minutes. A slight smell or taste of chlorine indicates that the water is fit to drink.

Iodine: This can be used in much the same way as bleach.

▲ *Use a sock, filled with sand if possible, to filter silt and debris out of your water before you purify it. Ideally, use fine sand at the bottom and coarser sand at the top.*

Water-purifying tablets: If you use commercial tablets, ensure you follow the package directions. They will make the water taste of bleach, but it will be very safe.

With all these agents, be sure to shake the container so that the purifier reaches every part of the water, to ensure that no bacteria are left behind. Bacteria often lurk in the screw top of a bottle, for example.

FILTERING WATER

1 To filter out pieces of debris and small aquatic creatures floating in water, hollow out a piece of dead wood by burning it almost through.

2 Create a form of sieve or strainer by stuffing the cavity with grass to catch the larger particles. The charcoal on the log will also help to clean the water.

3 Pour the water you have collected through the filter and collect it in a container placed underneath. The water will now need to be purified.

DESALINATING SEA WATER

1 When all you have is salt water, it's possible to make drinking water by distilling it. Bring it to the boil in a fireproof container.

2 Place a clean piece of cloth over the container so it catches all the steam. If you don't have any cloth, you can use moss instead.

3 From time to time, wring out the cloth or mosses and catch the liquid in another container. This water will be pure and ready to drink when cooled.

The problem with some of the above methods is that water treated in this way can make you feel unwell if you drink it over an extensive period of time. Many makers of commercially available tablets will advise you not to use their product continuously for longer than a few weeks. And, of course, tablets and tinctures eventually run out, so use them to extend the time before you have to gather clean water and purify it using more primitive methods.

COMMERCIAL FILTERS

The second option is to use a commercial filter. Such filters are an ideal way to clean large amounts of water over a long period. There are many different types of filters on the market, and many are small enough to fit in your pocket.

Filters are available for different conditions. Make sure that your filter can take care of chemical as well as viral and bacterial pollution, as it is possible to buy filters that filter out only one type of pollutant. Read the instructions carefully, as some filters require you to clean them regularly with iodine or similar fluids. Some filters have a shelf life too, meaning they can only filter a certain amount of water before "running out". If this happens you will have to fall back on the boiling method.

VITAL SALT

You can't drink salt water, but your body does need a regular intake of salt in order to retain water. So when you desalinate salt water, keep and use the salt that remains behind when the liquid has evaporated.

RESTORING THE TASTE OF BOILED WATER

1 When water has been purified by boiling for 15–20 minutes, it loses its taste. It will be perfectly drinkable, but will simply taste flat.

2 Adding a tiny amount of charcoal greatly improves the taste. You will need to let the water stand for a little while after adding the charcoal.

3 Another way of refreshing the water is to blow air through it using a straw. Alternatively, you can pour the water from container to container.

Further ways to find and treat water

Even in the most inhospitable, apparently arid terrain, it may be possible to find enough water to sustain life.

SEARCH FOR TRAILS

In the desert, it is often worthwhile following local wildlife to their water source, though you should keep in mind that a lot of desert animals do not drink, but get their liquid from the food they eat.

There is an important saying among the natives of desert regions: "The path is wiser than the person who walks it." Animals and native people use the same trails, and these paths often twist and meander across the land. If you come across such a trail it is better to follow it than to walk in a straight line to "cut off a corner". The trails follow courses where there are the least obstacles. Furthermore, they often run from shadow to shadow, and from water source to water source. If you find a well-used trail in the desert follow it, and stick to it.

UNDERGROUND WATER

In a dry region, look for dried-up river beds or canyons where water can be found by digging. Any vegetation will generally lead you in the right direction. The first plants you find will be thorny brush, farthest from the invisible water source; when the vegetation changes to grass-like plants you will be near the underground

▲ *Placing a clear bag over a leafy branch with one corner weighed down will collect water as it evaporates from the leaves and condenses on the bag.*

▲ *Some water filters can be complicated and contain a number of components (as with this tower water filter) and this may cause difficulties in extreme conditions.*

▲ *The tube of a portable filter goes into the unpurified water and clean water comes out of the spout once the pump is primed.*

▲ *Purifying agents can be used to eliminate any bacteria in water; their main drawback is their unpleasant taste.*

water. A ribbon of vegetation is often the only indication of a streambed in the desert, but it shows that there is water below ground. If the water is very hard to get at, you may be able to reach it with a filter straw, if you are carrying one. This very small, light device enables you to drink directly from an impure water source in an emergency, filtering and purifying the water as you suck it up.

In some deserts indigenous peoples have built extensive waterworks that capture any rainfall that does occur. In the Negev desert in Israel, for instance, there are areas where channels built in the rocks catch any rainwater that runs

down the hills and guide it to deep water pits. These systems are so effective that there will be water in the pits all year round. This may be valuable information if you land in a survival situation in a desert region where such pits exist.

COLLECTING CONDENSATION

An easy way to get water when the temperature is high and there is plenty of vegetation is to "capture" a branch with plenty of leaves, and tie a transparent plastic bag around it. Make sure you choose a tree that is non-poisonous, as the poison may find its way into the water. Then you must

MAKING A SOLAR STILL

1 To desalinate or purify water, build a solar still by digging a pit 60cm/2ft wide and 60cm/2ft deep. (Don't try to use a solar still to procure water in the desert, as it takes too much effort for too little return.)

2 Place an empty container in the middle of the pit to act as a collecting bowl. If you have a plastic tube at least 60–90cm/2–3ft long, place one end in the container, and allow the other end to come out of the side of the pit.

3 Place whatever water and vegetation you have found beside the collecting bowl. Place a sheet of clear plastic over the pit, secured by sand and weighted in the middle. Any condensation that forms will drip into the bowl.

---

tie one corner of the bag down, so the water doesn't escape near the branch where you tied the bag closed.

After a day, you can often procure a substantial volume of water by this means. Remember to change the location of the bag regularly to prevent leaves drying out completely, thereby stopping the process. A bag placed on a branch in the sun will produce more water than a bag placed in shadow.

The water produced by this method will be absolutely clean and safe to drink without any purification, though you may find that a lot of debris from the branch has dropped into the water. A quick filtering should sort that out.

WATER FROM SNOW AND ICE
In arctic regions, your main source of water may be the snow and ice around you. The snow is always as clean – or as dirty – as rainwater: that is, it may contain chemicals but not micro-organisms, though if it has been lying on the ground for an extended period of time it may have picked up pollutants from the environment. The saying "Never eat yellow snow" is one to be heeded.

Snow should always be pre-melted, as it takes too much of your body's energy to melt it in your mouth or in your stomach. This may not only cause you to lose vital heat, but can also lead

to dehydration, as you cannot get sufficient water into your system quickly enough.

Ice can be a great source of water, though again it will need to be melted. In arctic regions the problem is that a lot of ice is formed from salt water. Ice that is opaque or grey is often formed from salt water. More crystalline ice, with a bluish cast, has little or no salt in it. The water from salt water ice will need to be desalinated for drinking.

Don't forget that ice is no cleaner than the water it was formed from, and will often require purification. Some bacteria and viruses are able to survive for many years in a frozen state.

USING A FILTER STRAW

1 If you find a dried-up watercourse, you can dig down and use a filter straw to obtain the water directly.

2 It is possible to drink water direct from an inaccessible source if you have some kind of filter straw.

3 Before taking water from a pool try to clean the surface of the water or you will clog up your filter.

FOOD

When you begin to fend for yourself in the wilderness, it immediately becomes obvious how much is taken for granted in the modern urban environment. The food you normally eat probably comes with very little effort, whereas providing yourself with food in the wild is an activity and a chore that may consume a large part of the day. One thing is for sure: gathering all your food from the wild for a few days will make you appreciate your nourishment a lot more. Another facet you may notice is that you will have to adjust your taste buds. You become so used to the tastes of the foods you buy and cook that it can take a while to assimilate the different tastes and textures of the food that is available for free in the wild. However, when you are eating to survive you will quickly learn to appreciate your new-found sustenance.

Nutrition for survival

Food is our body's fuel. It supplies us with energy not only to work but to generate the heat that maintains our body temperature. Food also provides the body with the material needed to make and repair cells.

Activities such as hiking or climbing use huge amounts of energy, and if your energy levels are not topped up regularly, the body will start to use its reserves of energy, stored in the form of fat. This too will eventually run out, depending on how much fat your body contains. If your fuel supplies are still not topped up, your body will be less able to expend energy as it tries to maintain the supply to your vital organs. When all stored energy runs out, death soon follows.

THE CALORIES YOU NEED
The amount of energy you need in the form of food is measured in calories. A calorie is a unit of energy – the amount needed to raise the temperature of 1g of water by 1°C. Because this is a very small amount of energy, the kilocalorie (1000 calories) is more commonly used to measure food requirements, often expressed as a Calorie (with a capital C).

The amount of food you need each day varies with age, gender and the amount of energy you are expending.

▼ *Roots and tubers, such as these cultivated yams, provide essential nutrition. Your survival might depend on what grows below the ground when other foods are scarce.*

To function properly when working moderately, the average woman needs about 1500 Calories per day and the average man needs about 1800 Calories per day. However, in a survival situation you may be using as many as 4000–5000 Calories per day if you are working very hard (building your shelter, for instance) or trying to keep the body warm in extreme weather conditions. Foods rich in carbohydrates, such as fruits, vegetables and grains, normally supply the bulk of the body's energy needs.

VITAMINS
The body needs a regular supply of various organic substances, collectively known as vitamins, which are essential to break down foods into chemicals that can be absorbed and to sustain chemical processes within the cells. Deficiency diseases resulting from an absence of vitamins include scurvy (caused by a lack of vitamin C) and pellagra (a disorder of the nervous system caused by a lack of vitamin B3).

There are two different groups of vitamins. Those in the first group, notably vitamins B and C, are water-soluble and cannot be stored in the body, so they need to be replenished daily. The vitamins in the second group are fat-soluble and can therefore be stored in the body to be used over a longer period of time. They include vitamins A, D, E and K. These also need to be restored regularly, though not necessarily daily.

Like other essential nutrients, most vitamins can be obtained naturally by eating a balanced diet that includes fruit, vegetables, meat, grains and dairy products. This list can create problems in the wilderness, as you may not be able to get your hands on meat, grain or dairy products for a long time, while fruits, an excellent source of vitamins, are seasonal. The only vitamin manufactured in the body is vitamin D, which is essential for the absorption of calcium from the diet. This is created under the skin when in direct sunlight.

▲ *While locusts can destroy any vegetation they land on, they can also save your life as they make ideal food.*

▼ *Plantains are a staple food in the tropical regions of the world. They can be eaten green or ripe, raw or cooked.*

A BALANCED DIET

In normal circumstances, your daily diet should include foods from four groups, in the following proportions:
- Vegetables and fruits: 5–9 servings.
- Grain products, such as bread and cereals: 6–11 servings.
- Dairy products: 2–3 servings.
- Protein-rich foods such as meat, fish and beans: 2–3 servings.

▲ *In a survival situation you will have to work hard to keep yourself alive, so you need to find nourishing food to keep up your energy levels.*

KILLING TO SURVIVE

The two sources of food in the wild are plants and animals. Between them they provide the nutrition for survival. Plants are easy to gather but tend to be fairly low in food value, while animals take a lot of catching but are high in food value. For some, the idea of killing a living creature for food is completely at odds with their moral values, and even the most ardent meat-eater could find the experience of performing the *coup de grâce* on an animal fighting for its life a gruesome prospect. In a survival situation, though, you need to be able to deal with such issues from day one. Even then, the hunter must act responsibly and not cause unneccesary suffering.

▲ *Meat can be the hardest food to come by in the wilderness, since you need some kind of tool or trap, but animals provide a lot of protein and are an essential food.*

CELLULOSE FOR SURVIVAL

Grain products such as bread and cereals provide cellulose, otherwise known as fibre, in your ordinary diet. Your body is unable to break down cellulose, so it has no value as a nutrient. It travels through the body unchanged until it is eliminated as a waste product. It does, however, aid in the digestion of food, and is therefore an essential part of the diet. Deprived of cellulose, the body's system works too slowly and the result is constipation. When grains are not available, you should replace them by eating more vegetables, which also contain a certain amount of fibre.

▼ *Eggs are a good source of "complete" protein, an essential part of a balanced diet, but are only available in some seasons.*

PROTEIN AND CALCIUM

About 20 different amino acids are needed by the body to build other proteins that are not obtained from food. Of these, 12 are manufactured by the body and the remainder have to be obtained from food. Foods such as meat, fish, eggs and milk are known as "complete" proteins because they contain all eight of the essential amino acids we need.

Dairy products are an important part of a modern diet because they not only provide complete protein but are also a source of calcium. However, they are most likely to be unobtainable in a survival situation. Calcium can also be derived from water so milk can be replaced with extra water.

BALANCING A SURVIVAL DIET

In a survival situation where no grains or dairy products are available, the "balanced" diet (*see box opposite*) needs to be adjusted to include 11–20 portions of vegetable or fruit and 4–6 portions of protein-rich food, such as meat and fish, per day. Grains should be included if the opportunity arises.

Clearly, such a diet can bore the taste buds rather quickly, so it is important to learn to identify as many

edibles in the area as you can to create a more diverse diet. You should also seize every opportunity to collect seasonal items, such as fruits. When autumn arrives, spend as much time as possible gathering berries, for instance. Preserve them for winter by turning them into jams or drying them.

While you are gathering wild edibles, make a mental map of where you spot animals such as rabbits near their burrows. Consider where good trapping areas may lie, such as on an animal trail between a feeding and bedding ground and a water source. Just before dusk is a good time to locate them, or early in the morning.

▼ *Vegetables and fruits are most important in the wild, as they replace many of the foods we would normally eat.*

Edible plants

Since nearly three-quarters of your balanced diet in the wilderness will come from vegetables and fruit, your chances of survival will be improved by learning to recognize as many edible plants as possible. You also need to be able to recognize suitable plants at any time of the year, as many species look completely different in different seasons. For example, in a long-term survival situation you may be able to identify a tree that you know will bear fruit later in the year.

Some plants completely disappear in the winter except for the roots, which may provide essential nutrition when other foods are scarce. For this reason it can be important to locate particular plants while they are growing during the summer, or to recognize their likely habitat, so you can find the roots when you need them in the winter.

PLANT FOOD

Whenever you gather plants for food, whatever the species, keep the following points in mind:

- The plants should be clean and growing in a healthy looking area. Never collect plants close to roads, quarries and other disturbed areas.
- Never gather more than a third of a particular species in your area. You don't want the species to disappear, and you should keep some for real emergencies.
- When picking leaves and stems, try to find the youngest plants. In general they are easier to digest.
- Go for leaves that haven't been eaten away by other insects or animals. Always try to get the best quality food you can.
- Avoid accidentally gathering parts of other plants that are growing alongside those you are picking.
- Whatever plants you gather, eat them sparingly at first. People react differently to certain plants, and they may disagree with you.

TASTE TEST

Although about 80 per cent of plants are edible, and another small percentage are inedible but not poisonous, the remainder can be very dangerous. To avoid the toxic ones it is vital that you leave alone any plants you don't recognize. However, where there is no other option but starvation, you can do a taste test as a last resort.

Before you begin you should have eaten nothing in the previous eight hours. Divide up the plant so that the leaves, stem, roots, buds and flowers are separate, and test only one part of the plant at a time.

Start by smelling the first part of the plant: if it has a strong or acid odour, don't eat it.

Put the plant part against your skin for about 15 minutes (your elbow will do here). If there is no skin reaction, prepare it in the way you plan to cook it (boiling is a preferred method).

When the plant is cooked, place a small amount against your lip for a few minutes. If no itching or burning sensation occurs, place it under your tongue for about 15 minutes. If no

▶ *Doing a taste test is not recommended, but in an emergency it may be the only way to find edibles if your local knowledge is limited, and you will have to take the risk.*

▲ *Most people are aware of the tasty berries produced by plants such as blackberries and cranberries. However, other parts of the plants, such as the leaves, are also edible.*

burning or itching occurs, chew it well and keep it in your mouth for another 15 minutes. If there is still no irritation, you can swallow it.

Now you should wait for another eight hours to see if you still feel normal. If you start feeling sick or get an upset stomach, try to induce vomiting, and drink plenty of water. If

POISONOUS FUNGI

Fungi are rich in protein, high in vitamins, tasty and free to pick. There are over 1,000 edible species but you must only ever eat those you can definitely identify and know to be safe, as some contain deadly toxins, which can cause symptoms up to 14 hours after eating. It's a tough call when you're desperate for food but it's not worth death by liver failure.

Some poisonous species are easy to confuse with common edible mushrooms. A case in point is the yellow stainer, which will make you very ill, unlike its edible lookalike the horse mushroom (*Agaricus arvensis*). The yellow stainer colours yellow when pressed or cut, whereas the horse mushroom's cap keeps its natural buff colour. You should always make a positive identification before eating any fungus, rejecting any unfamiliar species, and all fungi should be cooked before eating.

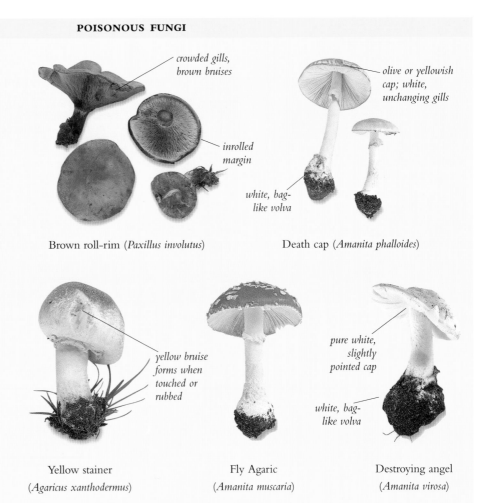

crowded gills, brown bruises

inrolled margin

Brown roll-rim (*Paxillus involutus*)

olive or yellowish cap; white, unchanging gills

white, bag-like volva

Death cap (*Amanita phalloides*)

yellow bruise forms when touched or rubbed

Yellow stainer (*Agaricus xanthodermus*)

Fly Agaric (*Amanita muscaria*)

pure white, slightly pointed cap

white, bag-like volva

Destroying angel (*Amanita virosa*)

all stays fine, prepare a little more for eating – you could try a quarter of a portion, for instance. Eat this and wait another eight hours. If there is still no adverse reaction, you can eat this part.

The problem with the test is that certain plants can make you seriously ill with just one leaf, while it is safe to eat others in small amounts, though they carry toxins that gather in your body, making you ill after you have eaten a large amount over several days. This is why it is best not to use it unless you have absolutely no other option.

While you are learning, your first few meals may be a little bland, but as you gain experience and expand your plant knowledge, you will soon be able to create tasty and satisfying meals in your "wilderness kitchen".

▼ *Pick only the plant you mean to pick: it's easy to grab leaves of a neighbouring plant, which could be dangerous, by accident.*

▼ *Be as picky as you would be when buying vegetables in a shop. Pick only young fresh leaves, and leave the half-eaten ones.*

▼▲ *In temperate climates wild foods such as rowan berries (above) and blackberries (below) are abundant in summer and autumn.*

Wildlife food sources

There is hardly any animal that cannot be eaten. However, for safety reasons it is important always to cook meat and fish thoroughly when you are taking your food from the wild, since this will kill bacteria, parasites and any other harmful organisms residing in the meat.

FISH AND SHELLFISH

If you have the time and energy to make some simple fishing tools or traps (*see page 98*), and there is flowing water close at hand, then fishing is a perfect way to get easy food. Fish are often plentiful and all freshwater fish are edible.

If you are on the coast, look in tidal pools and wet sand for marine edibles. Rocks on beaches or reefs leading into deeper water often bear clinging shellfish. Shellfish must always be caught alive, and should be cooked and eaten straight away. Avoid eating mussels in tropical zones in winter as they can be poisonous, and don't collect any fish in polluted areas.

▶ *Though crab meat is delicious, it must be eaten as soon as the crab is caught, as it goes off very quickly.*

▶ *Steam, boil, or bake shellfish in their shells. They make very good stews in combination with greens.*

▼ *Fishing can be an excellent way to gather fresh food. Especially when you can build fish traps that can be left unattended, fishing can be done with a minimum of effort.*

SMALL MAMMALS

If fishing is not an option, then you may need to catch smaller animals such as squirrels and rabbits. Rabbits can be found throughout the world and are relatively easy to catch – a snare or trap (*see page 96*) outside a burrow or along a rabbit run is usually enough to catch one. If you can make some tools for hunting, such as a throwing stick (*see page 100*) you can get larger animals such as deer this way. The only thing to look out for when getting food from land mammals is the danger an animal

▲ *Snails can be eaten, as long as they are boiled or cooked thoroughly. They are full of calcium, magnesium and vitamin C.*

may pose if it is not hunted correctly, or when it is wounded. Nearly all mammals will fight if they are cornered or protecting their young.

Hunting involves a host of different wilderness skills, including tracking, stalking and camouflage, and these are covered on the following pages. Learn these skills because in a survival situation you won't have the luxury of a rifle or ready-made bow and arrows.

Although most animals can be eaten, not all of them will necessarily be tasty or easily digested. Try to go for young animals, since their meat is usually the most tender. The flesh of some animals, although edible, may have a strong smell that can make it unpalatable. Though you will want to avoid such animals when possible, you should not disregard them as a viable food source.

INSECTS

The same goes for insects. In general, insects carry about 70 per cent of their weight in protein, while regular meat normally consists of about 20 per cent protein. The downside of eating insects is that you have to gather a fair number to get the same amount of meat as you would from, say, a rabbit. However, large quantities of insects can be found

GUTTING AND FILLETING A FISH

1 Insert the point of a knife or a sharp stone into the anal vent and slit the fish up the belly to just behind the gills. Carefully remove the internal organs.

2 Cut through the flesh just below the gills to separate the head, then open out the body and work the flesh away from the bones using your fingers.

3 Pull the head and bones away from the flesh in one piece, severing the spine at the tail end. The bones and head can be used to make stock.

by looking under stones, or in places where a lot of insects live in colonies, such as in rotten wood or anthills.

The only insects that you should steer clear of are adults that sting or bite, hairy or brightly coloured insects, and caterpillars and insects that have a pungent odour. You should also avoid spiders and common disease carriers such as ticks, flies and mosquitoes.

The idea of eating insects is enough to turn most people's stomachs. The best way to eat any unappetizing creature is to cook them in a stew, and try to forget they are even there.

▼ *Most frog species are edible, but avoid brightly coloured ones or those with a cross on their back. Most toads are poisonous.*

FORAGING FOR FOOD

Although you will certainly be making "normal" meals in your camp, you should try to use your energy efficiently and this may mean eating on the move, snacking on local edibles while you are finding materials for your shelter or tools. During the first few days, especially, it will be hard to make time to gather enough food for a proper meal – as long as you drink enough, you shouldn't worry about that. It is then best to feed by nibbling at nettles, berries and whatever else may be easy to find. Only when all

essential tasks have been taken care of should you take time to forage properly for food. If you have been prowling around the area for a few days, you should already have a good idea of where to go for what foods.

If you can source a regular supply of food, try to make your main meal around noon, when it is light enough to cook. In the evening, you can snack on leftovers or items that don't require cooking. Ordering your meals this way is also healthier for your body. A good meal in the morning will raise your energy levels, ready for the coming day.

▼ *Worms may appear unappetizing, but nearly all are edible. Put them in clean water for a few minutes, then mix into a stew.*

▼ *Rodents such as squirrels are abundant and will probably be the main part of your meat diet until you fashion hunting tools.*

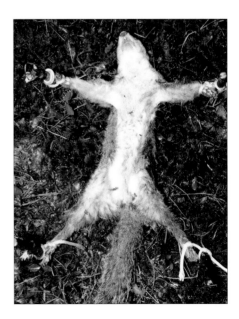

Tracking animals

When you start hunting animals for food the first thing you have to realize is that mammals and rodents – your potential meals – are not evenly spread about the whole wilderness. They gravitate close to where food, water and shelter are available. The middle of a dense forest, for instance, provides no water, light or food, so there will be few animals dwelling there. The edge of a forest is likely to provide food, water and shelter.

TRAILS AND RUNS

To find out which animals live in a particular area you must seek out their trails and runs. These are the most obvious signs of wildlife. Trails are used by many different species and generally lead towards water, food or shelter. Runs are smaller than trails, and are used by a particular animal species. They connect the trails with the shelter areas and sometimes connect water and food areas to the trails as well. Runs often change location, and sometimes a run becomes a trail over time. You can often guess by the width of the run who travels there.

SLEEPING AND FEEDING AREAS

The other signs that can help you establish your "virtual map" of animal life are sleeping, resting and feeding areas. Sleeping areas differ according to

---

THE *COUP DE GRACE*

When hunting you should always aim to kill with the first strike. If the animal is only wounded, once you've found it you need to finish it off swiftly. For an animal that's still dangerous, you will probably want to use your weapon again, but the most efficient method if the creature is safe to touch is to slit its throat either side of the windpipe. The best way to put a bird or small animal out of its misery is to break its neck by pulling the head away from the body with a sharp twist.

species. Many small animals sleep in burrows, while larger animals often sleep out in the open. If a sleeping area is out in the open you can usually detect the outline of the animal's body on the ground. These areas are often bordered by scrub that is dense enough to stop predators walking through, though not so dense that the animal can't look through the brush. They will have three or more escape routes.

Resting areas have less cover and generally offer animals a good view of their surroundings. They are often found near feeding and watering areas and are infrequently used.

Feeding areas are also likely to be different for different species, but they are often grassy areas with a good variety of plants.

IDENTIFYING SPECIES

Once you have these signs mapped out, you can try to find smaller signs to narrow down the species that live in the landscape. By looking more closely you can often find scat throughout the trails, runs, resting areas and even feeding areas. If there are hoofed animals, you can often find exposed roots and branches on the ground with scrape marks all over them. In feeding areas, you can observe how the grass and other plants are eaten. Rabbits, for instance, neatly scissor through grass,

---

▲ *A deer lie, or sleeping area, will be used for many nights, until the season changes or the area is threatened repeatedly.*

▼ *Clues such as these scrape marks on a mossy log help you to build a "virtual map" of an area's animal life.*

whereas hoofed animals rip it up, creating jagged breaks. In resting and sleeping areas you will no doubt find hairs belonging to the residents.

Next, you can look for actual animal footprints, narrowing certain runs and feeding areas down even further. Quite often, you won't actually find such clear prints as those shown opposite, but more of an outline. The tracks that you do find, whether they are outlines (compression marks) or full prints, should be combined with all the other information you have found on the trail or run, to give you a clear picture of which animal uses it.

IDENTIFYING ANIMAL FOOTPRINTS

Being able to read animal footprints is a great survival skill. Footprints reveal the identity of an animal, the direction in which it was heading and when it last used the track – all crucial information when hunting animals for food or keeping out of the way of animals such as bears or wild cats.

▲ **Grey fox**: *front foot 4 x 3.5cm/1⁵/8 x 1³/8in, rear foot 3.8 x 3.2cm /1¹/2 x 1¹/4in.*

▲ **Otter**: *front foot 6.7 x 7.5cm/2⁵/8 x 3in, rear foot 7.3 x 8cm /2⁷/8 x 3¹/8in.*

▲ **Skunk**: *front foot 2.2 x 2.8cm/⁷/8 x 1¹/8in, rear foot 3.8 x 3.8cm /1¹/2 x 1¹/2in.*

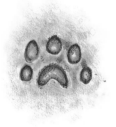

▲ **Marten**: *front foot 4.5 x 4.5cm/1³/4 x 1³/4in, rear foot 3.5 x 4cm /1³/8 x 1⁵/8in.*

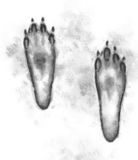

▲ **Hare**: *front foot 3.8 x 2.8cm /1¹/2 x 1¹/8in, rear foot 7.5 x 5cm/3 x 2in.*

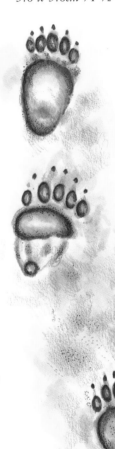

▲ **Rabbit**: *front foot 2.2 x 1.5cm/⁷/8 x⁵/8in, rear foot 7 x 2.8cm/2³/4 x 1¹/8in.*

▲ **Weasel**: *front foot 2.8 x 1.2cm/1¹/8 x ¹/2in, rear foot 3.8 x 2cm /1¹/2 x ³/4in.*

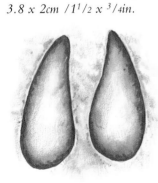

▲ **White tail deer**: *(one foot shown) front foot 7.5 x 4.7cm/3 x 1⁷/8in, rear foot 6.7 x 3.8cm/2⁵/8 x 1¹/2in.*

▲ **Grey wolf**: *front foot 12 x 10.8cm/4³/4 x 4¹/4in, rear foot 11.5 x 10.5cm /4¹/2 x 4¹/8in.*

▲ **Grey squirrel**: *front foot 5 x 3.5cm/2 x 1³/8in, rear foot 6.7 x 3.2cm /2⁵/8 x 1¹/4in.*

▲ **Grizzly bear**: *front foot 14 x 12.5cm/5¹/2 x 5in, rear foot 25 x 14cm /10 x 5¹/2in.*

Stalking animals

In order to get close enough to animals to hunt them, you will have to learn some techniques that enable you to catch them unawares. You won't have a high-powered rifle but a survival bow or throwing stick, and in order to get close enough to kill accurately with one of these, you'll need to approach to within 10–15m/33–50ft. This means you'll need to be able to move quietly and invisibly.

CREEPING LIKE A FOX
First of all, it is important to slow down and become more aware of your surroundings. You can achieve part of that by adopting the "fox walk".

The fox walk is a stalking style that would have been used by our ancestors. The idea is to take each step by leaving your weight on your standing leg, while you feel the ground with your free foot before putting it down. To do this, simply roll your foot from the outside of the foot to the inside, feeling what is beneath your sole. Once you are sure there is nothing sharp or noisy below your foot, you can put it down and move your weight on to your front leg. If there is anything painful or noisy

on the ground, lift the foot back up without putting your weight on it, and try another spot nearby. You need to be just as careful when lifting your feet as when putting them down to avoid cracking twigs or moving stones.

You will find that this method of walking is certainly very slow, but the main advantages are that you don't need to take your eyes off your surroundings to look down at the ground, it is very quiet, and you appear less of a threat to other animals because you are moving so slowly.

WIDE-ANGLED VISION
Animals usually see us before we see them. One reason for this is that we are so noisy and move quite fast. However, the other reason is that animals view their surroundings in a different way. Animals use wide-angled vision and this enables them to see all the movement around them.

The way we see the world is in a series of focused views. We take snapshots of our environment. This means there is a lot we never see at all, because we are focused on something else. However, we also have the ability

▲ *The throwing stick (see page 100) has the advantage that it is easy to pick up off the ground whenever you enter a survival situation. Carry it with you wherever you go in case you come across an animal that has not noticed you.*

to use our eyes in a less focused way, the way animals do. With practice you should be able to see all the movement that goes on around you, although everything will appear slightly blurred.

THE FOX WALK

1 Carefully lift the foot to be moved off the ground. Keep your balance on the leg that is taking your weight.

2 Move your free foot forward and gently bring it down, rolling it from the outside in over the ground.

3 If the ground is clear, lower your foot and shift your weight forward. Repeat, moving in a slow, fluid motion.

PRACTISING WIDE-ANGLED VISION

1 To learn to see all around you, go to a wide field or into a forest. Hold your hands out in front of you with your fingers pointing in, 30cm/1ft apart.

2 Look at both hands, but also at everything in between them. Slowly move your arms out to your sides, still looking at everything between them.

3 When your hands are at your sides wiggle your fingers, and you should see your hands again. While keeping this "view" slowly drop your hands.

4 Still in the same frame of vision, stretch out your arms again in front of you, but this time hold one hand below the other.

5 Move your arms apart again, one arm up and the other down, while seeing everything in between until you lose sight of your hands.

6 When you drop your arms, you should have a field of view about 180 degrees wide and 80 degrees high. You will instantly spot any movement.

A lot of people, when learning this technique, end up wandering around like zombies because they are trying so hard to retain their wide-angled vision.

Don't forget to move your head around – by doing this you can increase your total angle of view to 360 degrees. so you miss nothing. Then, as soon as you see some interesting movement, focus on it. If it turns out to be nothing of interest, go back into wide-angled vision and move on.

You will see a lot more wildlife on your walks through the wilderness this way, since every little movement will catch your eye.

A NEW WAY OF LISTENING

You can extend your listening skills in the same way as your vision. Follow the steps of the wide-angled vision practice in your head, but use your ears to try to hear everything, rather than just the most obvious sounds.

EXPERIENCING YOUR SURROUNDINGS

These techniques will make you far more aware of your surroundings, and will make it easier for you to spot any wildlife in the area. There is one more layer of awareness you can add to the three already discussed – feeling.

Become aware of the wind caressing your body, feel the muscles move in your legs. Feel the rain falling on your skin and clothes. When you put all these skills together successfully, you will become more attuned to your environment. Rather than just being aware, you will become part of your surroundings, allowing you to sense an animal almost before you see it.

Moving around like this in the wilderness will enable you to get much closer to the local wildlife. To get close enough to hunt them, however, you will need a few more skills: the skills of stalking and camouflage.

STALKING SLOWLY

The basic stalking technique is nearly the same as the fox walk – you feel the ground before you put your weight on it. This time, however, it is much slower. So slow in fact, that it is not noticeable that you are moving at all. An average step would take you about a minute. You might even try to disguise any further movement by moving only when your environment is "moving" – when leaves are rustling in the wind or trees are swaying back and forth. Not only does this method hide your movement, it may also cover up any sounds you make inadvertently. Try to keep your hands either in front of you or behind you to help break up the familiar human shape. In front is generally easier because you can hold your weapon there or use your hands to help lift up your leg.

The two stalks shown below are mainly used when there is plenty of concealing brush between you and the animal. A third method involves lying on the ground on your belly, with your hands beside your shoulders. Lift yourself about 10cm/4in off the ground on your toes and hands and move forward. Then slowly lower your body back down to the ground, move your hands and toes forward, and repeat the action. Any additional movements, such as standing, sitting, getting your weapon ready or swatting a fly, need to be done extremely slowly.

KEEPING YOUR BALANCE

A big problem when moving very slowly is balance. To avoid wobbling, bend your knees slightly while remaining upright. This enables you to keep a tight check on your balance. If you do lose it, try to correct it below the hip. If you correct with your upper body, the movement will surely alert any animals nearby.

STALKING ON ALL FOURS

1 Set out on all fours. Use your hands to feel for noisy material below you.

2 Place your knee exactly on the spot where you have just removed your hand.

3 Use this method to creep up when there is plenty of low brush.

MOVING SILENTLY

1 Make sure that any clothes you are wearing are well tucked in.

2 Ensure your body does not hook into any foliage.

3 Toes will catch in brush if you don't curl them when lifting your feet.

CAMOUFLAGE FOR STALKING

1 Rub white ash, from a cold campfire, into your skin to dull its shine. This will also help to de-scent you.

2 Apply charcoal on areas that would normally not be shadowed. Make the "pattern" as random as possible.

3 Break up your outline further using mud, again creating a random pattern of light and shade.

4 Use leaves growing in the area to "stamp" mud on to your skin.

5 Sprinkle forest debris over the muddy patches while they are still sticky.

6 Try to cultivate a "quiet mind" as you get really close to your prey.

USING CAMOUFLAGE

Camouflage is not about hiding, it is about being "invisible" right out in the open, so you can approach your quarry. If you are hiding behind a tree, it will be hard to launch an arrow or a throwing stick at an animal.

There are two simple ways to camouflage yourself. One is to rub white wood ash all over your body and clothes, then use charcoal to break up your appearance. Apply it to areas that would normally be light, such as right below your eyes and on the bridge of your nose. Use mud to paint different colours on your body. You should finish by rolling through some forest debris to "fluff up" your appearance, breaking your shape up even further. Because you have covered yourself in wood ash, your smell will also be well camouflaged. The second method is a lot easier. You simply roll in the mud, then in forest litter. Because your smell may not be adequately covered using this method, you may want to rub in some smelly plants. Use only species that grow in the area where you intend to hunt. If you use different plants your smell will still be obvious.

If you camouflage properly and apply good stalking and awareness, you should get almost within touching distance of most animals. To get really close, however, it is important to quieten your mind as well. Animals are very good at picking up your "vibe".

Mammals do not see colours, so even without camouflage you should be able to get close enough for a good shot, provided the animal doesn't smell you. That is, if there are no birds around. Birds do see colour, and birds are also the sentries of the wilderness.

▲ *It is important not to muddy yourself completely, as you will then be making the shape of your body more apparent. Instead, try to create a random pattern.*

Setting animal traps

Before you learn how to set traps, you need to know that it is illegal in most parts of the world to do this unless your life depends on it. This is because a trap can kill an endangered animal as easily as the most abundant species, not to mention the harm it could cause to bigger animals or even to humans.

The traps described here are simple to make, can be used in most situations and are designed to kill quickly and cleanly. There are many types of traps, but these are the most effective. Once you have set a trap, test it to make sure that you will not make an animal suffer unnecessarily. There is no excuse for an animal to limp away from a deadfall or choke to death on a snare.

When setting traps, try to disturb the area as little as possible so as not to warn any animals that something is up. You should also set your traps far apart,

because when one is triggered, all animals in the vicinity will go on high alert. Make sure they are well camouflaged by using wood ash, mud and strong-smelling local plants.

THE FIGURE-4 DEADFALL TRAP
This trap is intended mainly for feeding areas. It is called a "deadfall" trap because it works on the principle that a heavy weight will fall on the head of the animal when it nibbles on the food you place on the bait stick.

The simple trap described here is made of three sticks and looks like a figure 4 when set up. The arrangement is kept in place by the weight, but will collapse when the baited end of the horizontal stick is pushed by the animal. The weight of the deadfall should be about twice the weight of the animal you are trying to catch –

enough to kill it, but not so heavy that the animal will be completely squashed. The trap shown below would be an appropriate size to kill a rabbit.

You can make the trap more effective by placing an "anvil" such as a flat stone underneath. Make sure that the weight does not extend over the upright stick. If it does, it may fall on top of the stick rather than the animal.

Bait the trap with the plant that, from your observation, the intended victim seems to enjoy most. Be wary of importing a plant for bait, as animals may be suspicious of a plant that does not naturally occur in the area.

To force the animal to come in from the right direction, so that it pushes the stick when it eats the bait, you can build some sort of fence around the structure, though it must look natural and not arouse suspicion.

SETTING A FIGURE-4 DEADFALL TRAP

1 Square off the central part of the vertical stick and carve the tip to a flat "screwdriver" shape.

2 Near the end of the horizontal (bait) stick carve an upward-pointing notch to take the end of the diagonal stick.

3 Carve a slot to hold the bait stick against the squared-off section of the upright, at 90 degrees from the notch.

4 Carve a notch in the diagonal stick to take the top of the upright and sharpen the end to fit in the bait stick.

5 To set the trap, apply pressure on the diagonal stick while using the other hand to put the notches into place.

6 Lean a weight (such as a log or rock) on top of the diagonal stick and bait the free end of the horizontal stick.

SETTING A TWO-HOOK SNARE TRAP

1 Carve a notch near the top of a stick and plant it securely in the ground.

2 The second stick, also notched, will be tied to a flexible branch overhead.

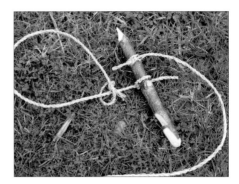

3 The loop the animal will walk into is also tied to the second stick.

4 Tie the second stick to the branch and hook the notches together. The fit should be secure but easy to set off.

5 Make sure the loop will slip easily and is the right size to fit over the animal's head as it walks through.

6 Rest the open loop on sticks or blades of strong grass, about two to four fingers' width above the ground.

THE TWO-HOOK SNARE TRAP

This snare trap is generally used on animal runs, though you can adapt it for use in feeding areas as well. It is important to ensure that the snare is strong enough to break the animal's neck and lift it high enough off the ground to prevent other animals getting at it before you do.

The trap consists of two sticks, each notched so they will hook into each other. One of the hooked sticks is planted firmly in the ground, while the other is tied with a length of cordage to a strong, flexible sapling or branch, which keeps the hooks together under tension. A slipknot loop is tied on to the hook attached to the string and placed over the run so that an animal walking into it will trigger the trap and be lifted up by the branch.

The height of the loop should be such that the animal will walk straight in. For a rabbit, for example, the correct height would be about a hand's width above the ground, while the loop should be about 12.5cm/5in in diameter. By varying the depth of the notches, you can change the sensitivity of the trap, depending on the size of the animal you are trying to catch. What you want to avoid is subjecting the animal to a slow death, so it's important to get the settings right.

Make sure you don't use green wood, since the two branches could fuse together – they can even freeze together during the night. You can increase the tension on the trap by using a number of saplings or branches in a row to compound their power. If there are no flexible branches near the run, you can make a lever and fulcrum by pounding a Y-shaped stick into the ground and tying a long branch over the top. Tie the string to one end of the lever and add a heavy weight to the other.

▼ *A lever and fulcrum can be made from sticks to support the two-hook snare trap when there is no suitable branch nearby.*

▼ *The two-hook trap can be adapted for fish by replacing the noose with fishing line. It must raise the fish well out of the water.*

Fishing techniques

If you are near water, fishing is an excellent way to obtain high-protein food. Fish can be netted, hooked, speared or snared, or even caught by hand. Setting a trap in a stream allows you to get on with other tasks while waiting for the fish to swim into it.

TRAPPING FISH

One of the easiest ways to catch fish is with a snare such as the two-hook trap described on page 97. You can adapt this by using fishing line in place of a noose, arranging it so that the fish is pulled well out of the water.

Another good method is to make a fish pen (*see below*): erect a curved fence to create an enclosure with only one opening facing upriver, then construct a funnel leading into the opening. If the stream is fast-flowing this may be enough to catch fish. In slower water, weave in flexible twigs so that they stick out towards the trap entrance. The sticks will bend aside as a fish swims in, but not when it tries to swim back out again. You can vary the size of fish the trap catches by adjusting the gaps between the fence poles.

MAKING A FISH SPEAR

If you want to catch larger fish and have enough time on your hands to be selective, making a fishing spear is the best option. The spear is made in two parts: a two-pronged spearhead is fitted into a notch in the end of a long, straight shaft. The reason for this is that if you miss the fish and hit the bottom of the stream, the spearhead will simply come out of the notch, whereas if the spear were made in one piece the prongs might break. The spearhead is loosely tied to the shaft so that it can be retrieved if it comes apart.

It is best to use green wood to make the spearhead as it has flexibility and will split without breaking. The stick should be completely straight and about 2.5cm/1in thick. It must be tightly wrapped with cord to stop it splitting too far, and the cord should be made of plant fibre, as sinew will loosen when it is immersed in water.

The prongs of the spear need to be sharp but strong, so that they will stand up to striking stones on the stream bed. On the inner surfaces of the prongs you will need to cut two small "shelves" to support barbs so that once speared the fish can't escape. The best materials for the barbs are sharp stones such as flint flakes or slivers of very hard wood. You can also easily make barbs from the bones of other animals. The barbs must be tied on tightly using fine cordage. If you know how to make pitch glue (*see page 124*) use it to make the joints between the barbs and wood more secure.

▲ *Spearing a fish requires clear water to spot your prey, stealth in stalking the fish then speed and accuracy in jabbing the spear.*

FISHING WITH A SPEAR

Look for a likely fishing spot – it could be on the outside of bends if it's cool, under shade on a hot, sunny day, in white water, or in shallows. Sit absolutely still, with the tip of the spear in the water, ready to stab a fish when it appears, or try stalking your prey. You'll need to experiment with different spots, times and styles until you are successful.

MAKING A FISH PEN

1 Erect a half-circle of sticks in fast-flowing water where fish are present, making sure the water flows into the opening in the "fence".

2 Create a funnel by planting more sticks to make two fences out to both banks of the stream, leaving a small opening where the fish can swim in.

3 In slower streams, weave some branches through the fences pointing towards the trap, so that the fish can swim in but not back out again.

MAKING A FISHING SPEAR

1 Find a straight stick about 30cm/1ft long and 2.5cm/1in in diameter and clean off any side-branches.

2 Wrap a length of cord made from plant fibre tightly around the central part of the stick.

3 Using a sharp stone, carefully split the stick. The binding will stop the split going further than the centre.

4 Wedge a small twig as far into the centre as possible to push the two "prongs" apart by 5–7.5cm/2–3in.

5 Use more cord to tie the wedge in place, to stop it popping out of the spear when the wood dries a little.

6 Using a knife or a sharp stone, carve the two prongs into long but sturdy points.

7 Carve a small "shelf" on the inside of each prong to support the barbs.

8 Use flint to produce two sharp flakes about 2.5cm/1in long for the barbs.

9 Using fine cordage, tie the barbs into place on the prongs.

10 Carve the other end of the spear-head into a flat plank shape. This will fit into a notch in the spear shaft.

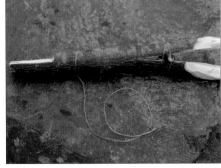

11 Tie a length of string to the spearhead and make a noose on the free end to tie around the spear shaft.

12 Carve a notch in the end of a straight pole 3–3.5m/9–12ft long and fit the spearhead on to the shaft.

Making and using a throwing stick

The first hunting tool you are likely to make and use in the wilderness is a throwing stick, which can be any sturdy stick you can find. It needs to be about 5–7.5cm/2–3in in diameter and about 60cm/2ft long. It can also be made into a quieter, faster weapon by carving the central section in the shape of a wing. You can even carve a non-returning boomerang, which may be accurately thrown over more than 100m/33yd. The principles are the same.

The throwing stick is mainly a tool for the opportunistic hunter. As soon as you are in a situation where food needs to be provided, you can simply pick up a suitable stick and carry it about with you wherever you go. It will be there when a curious animal pokes its head out of the bushes right in front of you. This way of hunting is particularly effective if you move around using the fox walk and wide-angled vision, as described on pages 92 and 93.

THROWING THE STICK
There are two common ways of throwing the throwing stick. The first method is overarm. Though there is less chance of hitting the animal, because the killing zone is only about 7.5cm/3in wide, this technique is very useful when there are many trees between you and the animal, or when you have to deal with high grass that

▲ *A throwing stick should be held so the butt end sits in the palm of your hand. It should not extend past your hand, as this could cause the stick to injure you, or the throw to go off course.*

would obstruct an underarm throw. One tip to remember is to give a flick with your wrist as you release the stick to give it extra revolutions, increasing the chance of hitting the target.

The second method is the underarm throw. The stick is held with its end in the hand in the same way as before.

▲ *Placing your thumb over the end of the stick ensures that it stays in the right spot in your hand. By holding the thumb like this, you can also achieve a throw in which the stick spins a lot while in the air.*

This time, however, you are standing sideways and the stick rotates horizontally through the air. This gives you a much better chance of killing the animal because the killing zone is about 60cm/2ft wide, but you can use it only when there is no grass or shrub to block the throw.

MAKING A THROWING STICK

1 Shaping the stick reduces the noise it makes in the air, and makes it fly faster. Find a sturdy but flexible piece of wood (yew in this instance).

2 Carve two sides of the stick, working it down to a wing-like shape. Try to orient any bend along the wing, so it does not affect the flight of the stick.

3 Leave more wood at the ends to provide some extra weight and so that you can easily sharpen the ends without the stick getting too weak.

USING A THROWING STICK OVERARM

1 If you are right-handed, place your left foot forward and hold the stick over your shoulder. Face the target.

2 You can use your elbow to aim roughly at your target. Start to throw the stick forward over your shoulder.

3 Just as you release the stick, give it a little flick with your wrist to produce extra revolutions in its flight.

USING A THROWING STICK UNDERARM

1 Stand sideways to the target, holding the stick at waist level.

2 Bring the stick behind you as you move your body forward.

3 Sink through your knees, resting your non-throwing hand on one knee.

4 Start to throw your hip into the throw as you crouch down.

5 Use your whole body to provide the power for the throw.

6 Flick your wrist just as you release the stick to give it spin.

Skinning and butchering an animal

Once you have managed to trap and dispatch an animal, it is important to hang and skin it as soon as possible. If the skin is left on for too long, the heat inside will spoil the meat rapidly. The internal organs should also be removed; they deteriorate quickly and any spillage of their contents will contaminate the meat.

If you are dealing with a large animal, such as a deer, hang it from a horizontal pole by its front legs and neck. If it is a small animal, such as a rabbit, lay it out on its back and tie all four legs to stakes so it is spread-eagled.

SKINNING THE ANIMAL

After making a small initial cut at the breastbone, insert your fingers to open it out so that there is no danger of puncturing the gut: from now on you can make sure your knife does not cut anything but skin. Push down under the skin with your fingers to create a

▼ *If you are in the wilderness for a long period, a deer provides not only good meat but also buckskin to make warm clothes.*

gap before cutting with your tool. Your cut should go all the way from the head to the reproductive organs.

With a large animal you should complete the skinning process before cutting into the flesh. If you have a small animal you can continue with the butchering, but if you decide to skin it fully now, make sure you are working on as clean a surface as you can prepare: it's amazing how forest debris always manages to get on to the carcass.

To continue the skinning, cut from the initial incision all the way up each leg, as far as you can go. Then finish off by cutting around the reproductive organs and the neck and by carefully cutting around the legs. (The leg tendons, or sinews, can be used in many ways. If you want to keep them, be very careful that you don't sever them when cutting around the legs.) With all cuts complete you can take off the skin. If the animal is spread-eagled, it is best to untie the legs at this point.

Try to avoid using your knife. In fact it is very easy to remove the skin entirely without using a knife, and this will prevent accidental cuts in the skin. If you don't use a knife, there will also be a lot less fat left on the skin, which will need to be removed if you intend to tan the hide. The easiest way is to pull the skin away from the animal with one hand, while you work the fingers of the other hand between the muscles and the skin.

BUTCHERING THE ANIMAL

Once the skin is removed you are ready for the next stage in the process. Carefully cut through the abdominal muscles, starting again at the breastbone. Make sure you do not puncture any internal organs at this point as this would spoil the meat.

Make this cut all the way to the reproductive organs. Now, you need to cut around the reproductive organs and the anus. This can be hard because the hips will be in the way. If you cut any tubes going to the reproductive organs or the anus, tie them off so they won't

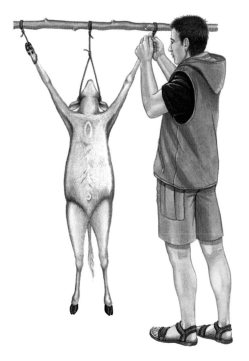

▲ *Hang a large animal by its front legs and head so that when the innards are removed they fall between the legs, minimizing the danger of contaminating the meat.*

leak into the meat. Now extend your cut all the way up to the windpipe. Once you reach it, cut through the windpipe and the gullet. If your animal is hanging by the front legs most of the internal organs should now fall out.

Now you can cut out the edible organs – the heart, liver, kidneys and lungs – and store them separately to avoid cross-contamination. Be careful not to puncture the gall bladder when removing the liver, as anything in contact with the gall will be spoiled.

WARNING

Ideally you should wear protective gloves when working with dead animals, as it is very easy to pick up an infection if bacteria from the meat get into small grazes or cuts on your hands. If you cannot get any kind of protection for your hands, try to make sure they are free of wounds and wash them at regular intervals, with soap or a disinfectant if possible.

HOW TO SKIN A DEER

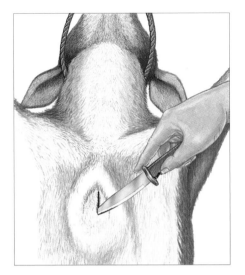

1 Start skinning by making a small, careful incision right over the breastbone to avoid piercing the gut.

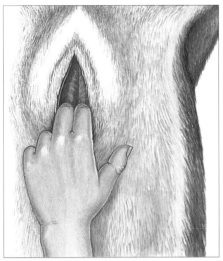

2 Insert two fingers, pointing down, into the incision to widen it and work the skin away from the flesh.

3 Insert your knife or cutting tool between your fingers, and slowly make your way down, cutting only the skin.

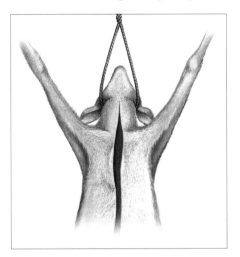

4 Stop at the reproductive organs, then do the same working upwards to the neck, starting from the initial cut.

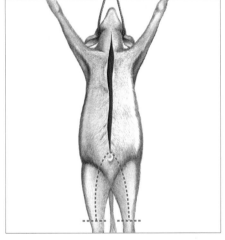

5 Cut through the skin around the hind legs, then cut down the fronts of the legs from the original incision.

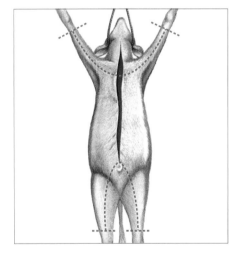

6 Do the same with the forelegs, cutting around the "wrists" and connecting these with the initial cut.

Check the whole carcass carefully for discoloration and other signs of spoilage. While you are working, you may find that a glaze seems to form over the meat. This is perfectly normal, and will even help to preserve it.

If you have not yet skinned a small animal, do so now. Otherwise, remove the legs and head and cook it as it is. For a larger animal, it is easier to cut off the meat while the carcass is hanging. Try to remove all the meat. Some parts, such as the ribs, have very little flesh, so it may be easier to cut the muscle between the ribs, break off the bones and fry them or put the whole ribs in a stew.

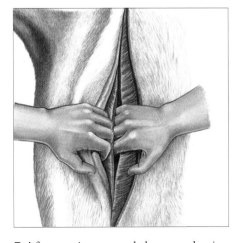

7 After cutting around the reproductive organs, anus and neck, you can pull off the skin. Next, deepen the cut on the breastbone until you hit bone.

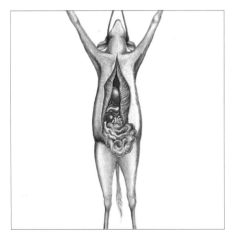

8 Follow the initial cut to open the body. Remove the edible organs and sever the windpipe, gullet and other connecting tubes to free the innards.

Preserving meat and other animal products

No part of an animal you have killed should be discarded. As well as providing fresh meat, the flesh of a large animal can be preserved for future meals, and the non-edible parts can be used to make clothes and tools.

USEFUL BODY PARTS

The intestines, stomach and bladder should be cleaned out immediately after butchering the animal, as they have many uses. The bundle of tendons should be carefully removed from each leg. Use a knife to open the bundle lengthways, then spread it out to dry.

The head of the animal contains lots of goodies. The liquid in the eyes makes a strong glue when mixed with resin. The tongue can be skinned and kept as meat. Keep the rest of the head intact for now. The brain can be eaten while fresh (within a day), but is better kept for tanning the hide later on.

Hooves should be kept as they can be boiled to make a strong glue. Skim the water they are boiling in to collect neatsfoot oil, used for softening hide.

DRYING MEAT

The easiest way to dry meat is in the sun or near a fire, but don't leave the meat too close to the fire, or it will fry, not dry. With bigger pieces of meat, you should remove any fat, which will go off quickly, then cut it into slices no

▲ *Antlers (if there are any) can be used for flint-knapping and other skills.*

▲ *The lower jaws of deer make great saws, though the teeth may loosen after a while.*

▲ *Clean and keep all animal bones because many of them can be made into tools.*

▲ *Either rinse animal bones well or bury them for a few weeks to clean them.*

more than 3mm/¹⁄₈in thick. Then you can hang these strips up around a fire or in the hot sun to dry. The meat must be fully dry before you store it. If it crumbles in your hands it may be a little too dry, but make sure that when

you bend the pieces of meat they crack. If they just bend without cracking, they are still too moist.

You can grind up this dried meat and store it for a long time in the intestines you cleaned earlier.

PRESERVING MEAT ON A TRIPOD

1 Find three poles about 120cm/4ft long and tie them together by wrapping cord loosely around the tops, then binding it tightly between them.

2 Place a number of horizontal poles around the frame you have made and bind them to the tripod at suitable heights to dry your strips of meat.

3 Cut the meat into strips as thin as you can get them. Place the tripod over the fire, making sure that the meat is not so close it cooks instead of drying.

Making buckskin for clothes

There is no material better suited to the outdoors than tanned buckskin. If you are to survive a long-term emergency, you may need to know how to make buckskin from animal hides so that you can make warm, durable clothing.

PREPARING THE HIDE

To start the process, make a framework that is about one and a half times larger all round than the hide you are going to treat. The framework should be strong and sturdy as the hide will be stretched on it. Two neighbouring trees make ideal verticals for the frame, and for the horizontals you can lash two strong poles across them.

Punch holes all round the hide so that you can tie it to the frame, but don't make them too close to the edge

as the cords will tear through the hide when it is stretched. Use strong cord for this, and check that the hide is taut.

You will need a sharp tool such as a knife or a sharp flake of stone to scrape the hide. Hold the tool so that the edge is at a right angle to the hide and draw it down while pressing into the surface. Make sure you are always scraping when pressing into the hide: if you stop the movement of the blade while maintaining pressure, you may punch through the hide.

SCRAPING

The purpose of scraping is to remove all the fat and the innermost layer of skin called the subcutaneous tissue (a layer of fat and connective tissue that houses larger blood vessels and nerves). Once the underside of the hide is

▲ *Leave the skin to soak in water mixed with charcoal, a tannic stream or a container of rainwater for a few days to loosen up the hair cuticles and any fatty tissue.*

scraped clean, start on the outer side and scrape off the hair and the outermost layer of skin (the epidermis). If the hair does not want to come off,

PREPARING AND SCRAPING AN ANIMAL HIDE

1 Tie two sturdy poles between two trees to make a frame one and a half times as long and wide as the hide.

2 Puncture holes about 7.5cm–10cm/ 3–4in apart all round the skin, about 2.5cm/1in in from the edge.

3 Tie the skin on to the frame, using a separate cord in each hole so that you can tighten each one when necessary.

4 Using a stone with a straight but not too sharp edge, scrape off all the fatty tissue and remaining flesh from the underside of the hide.

5 Using a very sharp flint, scrape off all the hair. If the skin has been soaked in acidic water it should come off easily. Scrape off the top layer of skin as well.

6 Scrape off any remaining fat on the underside of the hide and continue until the skin appears velvety. Leave the hide to dry out completely.

▲ *Part of the age-old process of making clothes from animal hides. When both sides have been scraped free of flesh, fat and hair, you are left with rawhide. To get buckskin for making clothes, the hide then needs to be tanned.*

then the skin may need to be soaked for a day or two in a stream or a container of water. Don't soak it for too long, or the hide may begin to rot.

When you have scraped both sides you are left with the dermis. Leave this stretched on the frame for a few days to dry out completely. At this point, you have created a fine grade of rawhide, which can be used for a multitude of purposes. To soften it for clothing, the hide needs to be tanned, and for this you can use the brains you saved when butchering the animal.

BRAIN-TANNING

Once the hide is dry, heat up some water and mix in the brains. Massage this mixture deeply into the hide. You can use egg-yolk for this job (if you have found birds' nests) as an alternative to brains, but in either case make sure the entire hide is saturated with the mixture. You can even take the hide off the rack, and soak it in the mixture in a container for a while.

The brains will stop the fibres binding back together to form rawhide, but only if the fibres are stretched apart while they dry. So the secret of soft buckskin is to stretch the fibres while the hide is drying. One way of doing this is to stake the hide out again and poke it with a rounded stick. Or you can hold it in your hands and stretch and pull it out until it is dry. If you can feel hard areas, you can try to give them some extra attention, though you may have to tan these sections again when the hide is completely dry. Once the whole hide is dry and soft, buff it over a tree trunk or a twisted cord to produce a material much like felt.

SMOKING THE HIDE

The next step is to smoke the hide. This is very important to stop your hide reverting to rawhide as soon as it gets wet. Sow the hide together to form a bag. Set a tripod above some embers and suspend the hide over it in such a way that the smoke has to travel through the hide. Now add smoky materials such as pine needles to the embers, and leave it for a few hours. Make sure the embers do not burst into flame, as this would ruin your hide. Once one side is fully smoked, turn the

BRAIN-TANNING AN ANIMAL HIDE

1 Having left the skin to dry completely, warm the animal's brains and massage them into the skin.

2 Pull the skin to stretch the fibres, continuing the process uninterrupted until the hide is completely dried out.

3 When the hide is dry and flexible you can soften it further by running it over a taut string or a branch.

bag inside out and smoke the other side. The finished product is buckskin, and is ready to be made into clothes.

You will need to re-smoke the hide once in a while to ensure it stays thoroughly oiled and prevent the fibres going hard again.

THE BENEFITS OF HIDE CLOTHING

Making clothes and other items from what is around you may be essential for long-term survival. Though it takes a lot of work to make a piece of soft buckskin, you will find that leather made this way is much stronger and more durable then modern leather. It is a natural product and therefore helps to mask your smell when stalking. It is also ultra-quiet and one of the best backgrounds for a camouflage pattern.

When making clothes, you can use various materials to sew hides together. Animal tendon could be used, though that would be more applicable in drier regions. You can also use cord made with plant fibres, though you may have to replace some of the seams from time to time. The easiest method is to tie the seams together using small strips of tanned hide made from offcuts. You can also use these for fringing, to help break up your outline in the bush. Make the fringing a little irregular and not too long, or it may snag in brush. The disadvantage of fringing is that it can show up your movements while stalking if you are not careful.

▼ *A small deerskin is easily big enough to make a pair of shoes following this pattern. If you have thick and thin skins, use the thicker skin for the soles.*

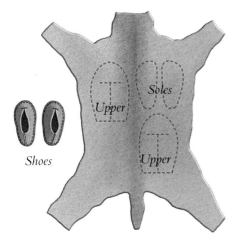

Shoes   Upper   Soles   Upper

TURNING SKINS INTO CLOTHING

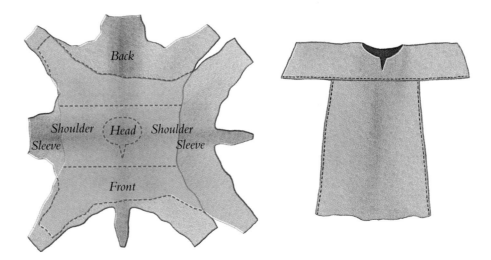

Back

Shoulder Sleeve   Head   Shoulder Sleeve

Front

▲ *Two average skins can make an excellent shirt, using them as shown above. This design gives extra material on the shoulders, making the shirt stronger and warmer.*

▲ *This is what the shirt would look like when it is finished. You could add fringing to the sleeves and hems to make your shape less obvious when stalking game.*

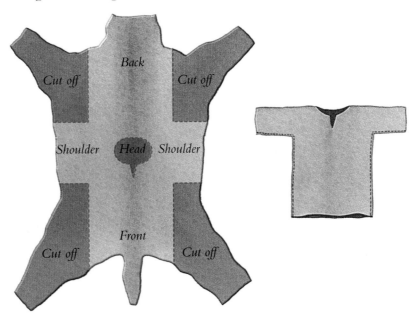

Back

Cut off   Cut off

Shoulder   Head   Shoulder

Front

Cut off   Cut off

▲ *If you have a large hide, you can cut the whole shirt out in one piece, one half becoming the front and the other becoming the back. Simply fold it at the shoulders and sew up the sides and sleeves.*

▲ *This shirt might feel a little "square" due to the fact that the sleeves are not shaped. It is a good idea to make the shirt very roomy, allowing plenty of material under the arms so you can move in it easily.*

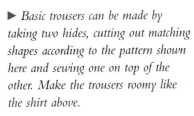

▶ *Basic trousers can be made by taking two hides, cutting out matching shapes according to the pattern shown here and sewing one on top of the other. Make the trousers roomy like the shirt above.*

TOOLS AND EQUIPMENT

One of the most satisfying aspects of survival in the wilderness is the making of tools and equipment. This often signals the end of sheer survival and the beginning of "living". Your existence is no longer a matter of primitive survival: many of the skills required to make tools from materials found in the wild are highly advanced techniques, which most modern people are not able to reproduce without re-learning and a lot of practice. These skills are truly a joy to learn, and many of them may lead you into a lifelong journey towards artistry and the perfection of, and even addiction to, wilderness survival skills.

Basic food bowls and containers

Using fire, you can very quickly turn out wooden bowls and spoons, simply by allowing an ember to burn into the wood in a controlled way.

To make a bowl, start with a thick log about 30cm/12in long (burn it to size if necessary). Split it in half then place an ember right in the centre of the flat side. By gently blowing on it, you can get the fire to spread slowly into the wood and also control the direction in which it burns. If you find you are getting too close to the side or bottom of the log, put some sand or clay over the spot to stop the ember

▼ *The stomach of an animal makes a watertight container and can be used to cook food and boil water in.*

▲ *Bark baskets are relatively easy to make, and can be used to hold a variety of items, such as equipment or edible plants.*

spreading that way. Scrape the surface clean of char regularly, as it will insulate the wood and make the burning process less efficient. If you want to speed up the process – and avoid hyperventilating – it is a good idea to use a straw made from a hollow stem such as elder, reed or bamboo, or the windpipe of an animal. You can use your burned-out bowl as it is, though you may find that food tastes better if you take time to scrape out all the char and sand the inside smooth.

Spoons can be made in exactly the same way as bowls, then carved to make them comfortable to eat with. Wooden utensils hold food particles in the fibres, however, so after washing them it is a good idea to hold them above a flame for a minute or two to sterilize them each time they are used.

▲ *Burning into wood is an easy way to produce containers, and has even been used to produce large items such as canoes.*

BARK CONTAINERS

Great containers can also be made from bark. Many different species, such as birch, cedar and elm, are suitable. Try to take it from trees that have fallen or are on their way out. If you have to take bark from a healthy tree, take a strip from only a third of its circumference to ensure that the tree survives. For best results, soak the bark in water for a few hours.

ANIMAL PRODUCTS

You can use the stomach of an animal to hold food or water. Clean it out, turn it inside out and suspend it from a tripod, or dig a hole in the ground and stake the edges around the pit. It can be used for boiling liquids by adding hot rocks. A bladder will work in the same way, though not for so long.

MAKING A SPOON

1 Light a good fire to make a large pile of embers. If necessary, shorten the stick you want to use in the fire.

2 Using tongs, place an ember on the flattened stick, on the point where you want your depression to form.

3 Hold the ember down and blow at it so that it burns into the wood. Sand out the depression and carve the spoon.

MAKING A BOWL

1 Make a sizeable fire in order to obtain plenty of embers for burning.

2 Split a log in half using a stone wedge and a sturdy branch hammer.

3 Place an ember on the wood, right in the centre of one half of the log.

4 Hold the ember down and blow on it gently. A depression will slowly form.

5 As the depression deepens, add more embers to burn the hole more quickly.

6 If you burn too close to one side, add clay to protect it from the fire.

MAKING A BARK BASKET

1 Select a strip of bark about 60cm/2ft long by 30cm/1ft wide.

2 Score an oval shape in the centre of the bark. Do not pierce the outer layer.

3 Using a sharp stone, punch holes all around the edges of the bark.

4 Bend the basket into shape and stitch the sides together tightly using cord.

5 To reinforce the basket, bind some stems into a ring to fit the rim.

6 Sew the ring into place using the holes you punctured earlier.

Weaving a basket

A basket can serve you in many useful ways, both for collecting and for storing food, and baskets can be made in a wide variety of forms, shapes and sizes. Once you have learned the technique you can use it to make containers of any size you need.

Basketwork allows air to circulate easily, so it is ideal for holding delicate wild foods such as berries and fungi, which deteriorate very quickly if they are carried in airtight containers. Baskets are also useful for storing wild greens or pieces of meat, or for gathering small-scale materials for kindling and tinder in the woods. A very loosely woven basket can also be used for trapping fish or to scoop small fish out of the water by hand.

MATERIALS FOR BASKETS
The function of each basket should dictate its size and shape, and may also influence the material you choose to make it from. Many different materials can be used to weave baskets, as long as they are flexible. The long, slender shoots of willow and hazel are traditionally used for basketry, and would be a very good source if they are growing in your vicinity, but there are plenty of other flexible materials that can also be used, such as pine or cedar shoots, spruce roots or cordage. Long shoots reduce the need to weave in new strands and make it easier to achieve a smooth, even finish.

▼ *A small collection of baskets of various sizes is useful for collecting food and keeping small items of all kinds safe.*

WEAVING A BASKET

1 Gather six flexible willow or hazel twigs to make the ribs of the basket.

2 Split one stick in the centre by inserting a cutting tool and twisting it.

3 Insert one of the other sticks into the split you have just created.

4 Place two more split sticks beside the first, and insert the remaining sticks.

5 Push two strands of weaving material into the splits alongside the three ribs.

6 Tightly weave one of the strands over the first three ribs. Hold at the bottom.

7 Weave the second strand under the first ribs, and over the second three.

8 Repeat to go around the centre three times. Make sure the weave is tight.

9 Now continue to weave between the individual ribs until you feel the base is big enough. Keep the shape circular.

10 Split each rib, right at the edge of the weave, twisting the tool as you bend it up to stop the rib breaking.

11 Repeat to bend all the ribs up, then place three weaving strands to the right side of one of the ribs.

12 Take the first strand and weave it over the first rib. Hold it in place at the bottom of the basket.

13 Weave the second strand under the first rib and over the second. Release the first strand and hold the second.

14 Weave the third strand under two ribs and over one rib. Release the previous strand and hold this one.

15 Continue weaving, following the last step, until the ribs are pointing upwards to your satisfaction.

16 When a strand runs out, lift it up and insert a new one in its place, so that it points in the same direction.

17 When the ribs are pointing up, continue using only two strands, following the weave used for the base.

18 When you have reached the height you want, tuck the ends of the strands into the previous rows.

19 Weave in the ribs if possible, or cut them off, leaving the ends protruding a little so that the weave doesn't slip off.

20 This weaving pattern will produce a strong basket of any size, even if its shape is not completely regular.

Crafting simple pottery

Pottery was the first craft to be developed in most human cultures, and serviceable pots are still made using natural river clay and the simplest of crafting and firing techniques. Your own containers may be crude but they will make effective utensils for cooking and eating.

FINDING THE CLAY

You won't have the luxury of buying ready-made clay in a survival situation but as it's an abundant natural material you should be able to find some to hand. Formed primarily by the weathering of granite, clay can be found all around us and the best way to look for pure, clean clay is by digging in a bend in a river, where the finest particles have settled.

PREPARING THE CLAY

Having gathered your clay, leave it to dry, then grind it to a powder so that you get rid of stones and any other impurities that would spoil the pottery. Once you have a fine clay powder, you should temper it by adding a little harder material, such as ground seashells, sand, powdered eggshells or

▼ *The thumb-pot technique can be used to make vessels such as bowls and lamps.*

crushed pottery fragments. Tempering the clay will prevent the pottery shrinking too much during drying and firing, thereby helping to prevent it cracking. Once the temper is mixed in, you can add water.

Knead the clay thoroughly before you start to shape it to eliminate any air bubbles, which would expand during firing and break the pot. Try to get the consistency of the clay right before you start working with it. The clay should be soft enough for you to move but

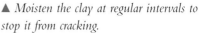

▲ *Moisten the clay at regular intervals to stop it from cracking.*

firm enough so that it does not stick to your hands. You'll soon get an idea of the sort of "give" you need to achieve in order to be able to craft simple pots.

FROM BALL TO BOWL

The pottery bowl described opposite uses a ball of clay about the size of an orange. It is simply shaped using your hands, using a pinching technique. Press in with your thumb as you turn it until you are about 6mm/^{1}/4in from the bottom, then start pressing outward, working from the bottom up, to form a pot. If the pot gets too big, put it on a flat surface while you thin the sides to a uniform 6mm/^{1}/4in. Once the pot is finished, leave it to dry for a few days.

Fire your pots after drying to make them more durable. The simplest form of firing, which is still practised by village potters in parts of the world today, is with open fires or with pits using a local source of fuel. The method used here is as basic as it comes. The firing temperature will be low, so your pots will eventually start to disintegrate, but you can easily make more to replace them.

MAKING A POTTERY BOWL

1 To make sure the clay is entirely pure, it is best to dry it and then pound it with a large stone.

2 You can then filter out any debris. Keep pounding until you have a fine clay powder.

3 Mix the powder with a small amount of temper such as crushed shell, adding about one part temper to ten parts clay.

4 Add just enough water to the powdered clay to make it hold together in a ball without breaking.

5 Knead the clay thoroughly, working it between your hands to smooth it and eliminate any air bubbles.

6 After kneading, shape the clay into a ball. For a small bowl you will need a ball about the size of an orange.

7 Press your thumb into the top of the ball, then turn it and repeat.

8 Keep turning and pressing, slowly widening the hole and shaping the pot.

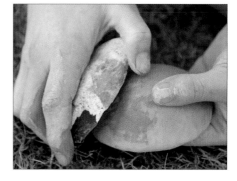

9 Dry for a few days, then burnish the pot with a stone to make it watertight.

10 To fire the clay, place the pot under a thick layer of soil and light a fire on top, or build a fire around the pot.

11 Make sure the flames are well away from the pot at first, and slowly get closer, so it doesn't heat up too quickly.

12 Once the pot is immersed in flames, add more wood and let the fire burn as hot as possible for about three hours.

Making a bow for hunting

A bow is a versatile hunting weapon that will allow you to stalk and kill mammals of any size. The bow described here is designed for short-term survival and is sometimes called a father-son bow, because it actually consists of two bows – a bigger bow with a smaller one tied on to the back. The reason for this construction is that the bow is made from green wood. Though this is easier to carve, it does not have the same strength as a bow made from properly seasoned wood. By adding a second stave, you can achieve a stronger bow with weaker wood.

WORKING WITH THE WOOD

To make the survival bow you will need a branch of a young tree without side branches or knots. The wood should be straight, about 150cm/5ft long with a diameter of 7.5cm/3in.

You will need to split the branch exactly down the centre of the wood as both halves will be used. If you don't manage to salvage two staves from the branch, cut another length and split it to obtain the second stave. In this case it need only be about 120cm/4ft long.

Once you have two staves, select the one that is going to become the "father" or main part of the bow. The side with the bark on will be the back of the bow, and this should never be touched with a knife. The other side, which will face you in the finished bow, is the belly. Measure off a handle

FLEXIBLE WOODS

The best woods for a bow are those that are flexible, such as hazel (although nearly all types of wood can be used for this survival bow). You can test the flexibility of wood by taking a small twig from a tree and bending its ends together. If it snaps cleanly, the wood might not be good for a bow. If it doesn't really snap, but breaks or bends with a lot of fibres, then you have a wood that will work well.

about 7.5cm/3in long in the centre of the bow, then carefully thin both limbs by carving until they start to bend evenly, forming a D-shape.

SHAPING AND TESTING THE BOW

At this point you can carve two notches at the end of each limb, and string a length of cordage between them. This is not the final string and doesn't have to be tight, but you can use it to pull the bow to see the result of your thinning more clearly.

The best way to do this is to make a "tillering-stick" about 75cm/30in long. Carve a notch on top of the stick and further notches every 12.5cm/5in. Sit the handle of the bow on the notch at the top and pull the string down to the first notch. Examine the bend of the bow. If it looks good, pull the string to the next notch. If you find spots that bend more then the rest, you need to thin the bow at either side of that weak spot so it bends evenly again. If parts of the limbs bend less than the rest, you'll need to thin those down a little more. Using this process to test the bow, keep thinning until you reach the last notch.

Now shorten the bowstring so that it is about 15cm/6in away from the handle when the bow is strung and

▲ *Though the "father-son" bow is made from green wood, which is weak, the two bows reinforce each other to give enough power for a kill.*

repeat the process until your bow has a draw of 63–70cm/25-28in. Use the same process to make the shorter bow, which needs a draw of 25–37cm/ 10–15in. The shorter bow will not need a handle. Once it is tied on to the back of the larger bow it should be "recurved" by pushing in two wedges on each side of the handle and tying them in place. Connect the limbs of the two bows and fit the string back on to the main bow. Each bow should bear a pull of 7–9kg/15–20lb.

FIRING THE BOW

Once you've made your arrows (*see following pages*) you can use your bow, though its performance will be greatly improved if it is left to dry out for a week or two. Don't expect instant success. Find some open ground (so that you don't lose your arrows), set up a target and start practising. Learn how to load, draw, aim and fire effectively from a range of distances. Once you are hitting the target with confidence it's time to go out and do it for real.

MAKING A SURVIVAL BOW

1 Gather two pieces of straight, flexible green wood, looking for poles without side branches or knots.

2 Split one branch in half using a stone wedge or other splitting tool. Always work away from the "back" of the bow.

3 Unless you have managed to split the branch exactly in half, repeat the procedure with the second stick.

4 The short bow should be about three-quarters the length of the main bow.

5 Carefully carve away to get an even bend along the stave.

6 With one stave completed, repeat for the second bow.

7 Carve two sets of notches in each end of the larger bow and one set of notches in each end of the smaller bow.

8 Tie the two bows together at the centre, with the belly of the smaller bow touching the back of the larger bow.

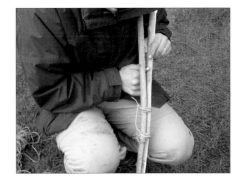

9 Insert wedges as close to each side of the handle as possible to "recurve" the smaller bow away from the larger bow.

10 Tie these wedges into place very securely to stop them popping out again when the bow is in use.

11 Tie the tips of the larger bow to those of the smaller bow. Make sure the connection is taut but not too tight.

12 Finally, string the main bow. The bowstring should be 10–12.5cm/4–5in shorter than the large bow stave.

Making arrows

It is best to make a number of arrows at a time, as they are easily broken or lost in use. Look for young shoots to make the shafts as they are firm and straight. Once the bark has been stripped off, the stems should be about 6–10mm/¹/₄–³/₈in thick. Cut them to a length of about 70cm/28in. Shoots of hazel, willow and yew all work really well for survival arrows.

If the shafts needs straightening, you can do this by heating the wood over the fire until it is just too hot to touch, then bending it in the opposite direction and holding it in that position until the wood has cooled down. When you let go, the bend should be gone. If it is not, repeat the process.

If you do not have any feathers to use as fletching, you can fletch the arrows with tough leaves, or tie a bunch of pine needles on to the shaft.

STRENGTHENING THE TIP

If you need to use your arrows quickly, you can get away with carving the shaft to a point and fire-hardening the tip after you have finished the fletching. If you have a little time on your hands, it is better to strengthen the tip of an arrow by notching it and inserting an arrowhead. Simple arrowheads can be made of bone or very hard wood, but you can also make arrowheads from stone. In any case, the arrowhead should be tied on securely.

To make it extra strong, coat the arrowhead with pitch glue (*see page 124*) before you tie it on to the shaft. Now all you have to do is wrap just behind the arrowhead to prevent the shaft from splitting, and wrap the shaft just in front of the notch in the back to prevent the string from splitting the shaft when the arrow is fired.

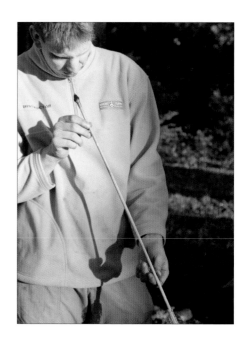

▲ *A "primitive" arrow should be made as straight as any modern arrow, otherwise it may miss the mark.*

SHARPENING AND SHAPING A FLINT ARROWHEAD

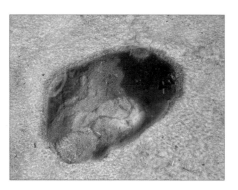

1 When you have found a suitable flake of material, imagine the arrowhead inside to help you shape the stone.

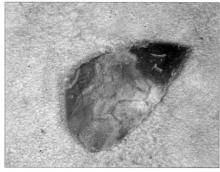

2 It is most important to thin the piece as much as possible while taking as little material as possible off the sides.

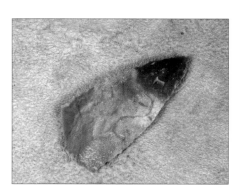

3 You should get to the required shape slowly but surely, so that a minimum of material loss is incurred.

4 When the piece is between 3–1.5mm/¹/₈–¹/₁₆in thick, it is thin enough for an arrowhead.

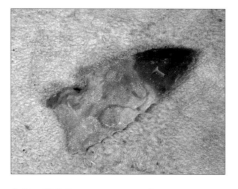

5 Small flakes are removed to create a notch. It is best to make the first notch on the most difficult side of the piece.

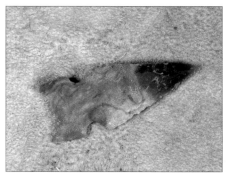

6 The second notch is made to match the first. After further sharpening and shaping, the arrowhead is ready for use.

MAKING AN ARROW

1 Find a young branch that is nearly perfectly straight with no side shoots.

2 Carefully strip off the bark. Don't cut into the wood, as that will weaken it.

3 Remove any bends by heating the wood and bending it the opposite way.

4 Cut a notch in one end to fit on to the bowstring, and a deeper notch in the other end to take the arrowhead.

5 To prepare deer sinew for binding the arrow, take a dried leg tendon and pull off long fibres.

6 Chew the fibres to make them supple and sticky: sinew sticks to itself when wet and shrinks and hardens as it dries.

7 When the sinew is soaked through, use it to bind the shaft just behind the notch to prevent splitting.

8 Repeat at the other end. Make sure the wrapping overlaps, because the sinew will stick only to itself.

9 Place a resin-soaked arrowhead in the notch, as deep as it will go. Make sure you orient it straight along the shaft.

10 Melt more pitch glue and mould it over the arrowhead so it "flows" into the shaft, to give smooth penetration.

11 When the glue has nearly set, wrap the arrowhead in place using more sinew to form an unbreakable bond.

12 Use sinew to bind on the fletching to balance the arrow – a half-stripped branch of spruce has been used here.

Making basic stone tools

Being able to make stone cutting tools is an important survival skill in this modern age. We are not allowed to carry knives on public transport, so after a crash, for example, you might find yourself in a survival situation without one. You may also want to learn the techniques out of interest, or as a way of connecting with the past.

The simplest way to produce a cutting tool is by "bipolar percussion". For this you need a rounded pebble about 7.5cm/3in long, preferably fine-grained or even glassy (coarse stone will not produce a sharp edge). Hold it on a stone anvil or pack sand around it to hold it upright. Now smash a heavy rock with all your strength down on the pebble. If you hit it hard enough, the stone will fracture into long, sharp shards that can be used as emergency cutting tools.

KNAPPING STONE

For more refined tools, a technique called "knapping" is used. Creating a tool from a stone is very much like chess. You have to learn the individual moves and put them all together to remove the right flakes.

Because the flakes you are working on are extremely sharp (obsidian can be 400 times as sharp as surgical steel) it is vital to protect yourself. This means

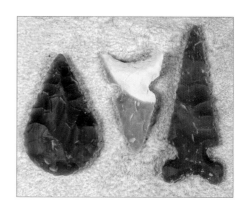

▲ *Arrowheads come in all shapes and sizes, depending on the use of the arrow as well as the skill of the knapper, but their principle task is to reinforce arrows, so beauty comes last. Even a simple flake could do the job.*

FLINT KNAPPING PROCESSES

1 For large pieces of flint, "direct percussion" is used. The "core" is often held on the outside of the leg and the flake is struck off with a stone.

2 When large, thin flakes are needed a "soft hammer" (in this case a piece of antler) is used, and the blow is angled in the direction of the flake.

3 The final method, "pressure flaking", is used to remove small flakes with precision, pressing outwards with a fine piece of antler to push the flakes off,

MAKING A WORKABLE KNIFE FROM STONE

1 Select a fine-grained pebble roughly the size of an egg, and a solid hammer stone at least twice as heavy. Steady the pebble on a sturdy rock surface.

2 Keeping your fingers out of the way, or using sand to hold the pebble upright, strike it as hard as you can with the hammer stone.

3 Ideally the pebble will split into a number of sharp-edged flakes. Even if it does not, you will often end up with at least one sharp piece, as here.

▶ *This hammer was produced by "pecking" a groove around a hard stone. A piece of hazel, shaped to fit the groove, forms a handle, which is strengthened with rawhide.*

wearing gloves, and using sheepskin or a large pad of leather when working on your lap. You should also wear safety goggles when practising as splinters may fly towards your eyes. If you take up knapping on a regular basis, make sure you do it in a well-ventilated area, preferably outside. Put down a groundsheet and clean the floor and all surfaces well after knapping so that no sharp debris is left lying around.

From an archaeological point of view, you should dispose of your flakes and chips (known as "debitage") responsibly. Some people bury a glass bottle beneath them to show any future digs that the flakes are not prehistoric.

▼ *Stone tools and arrowheads can be made from different types of stone. The top arrowhead is made from English flint, while the bottom one is of porcelanite.*

PREDICTING HOW STONE WILL FLAKE

There are five main "rules" to help you decide where flakes will come off a stone you are knapping:

- **The angle of the platform** The platform is the surface to which you are going to apply a force to detach a flake. An angle close to, but less than, 90 degrees in relation to the surface where the flake is to come off, gives the best result. An angle far less than this will result in a crushed edge, while more than this will produce nothing at all.

- **Every stone has an imaginary centre line** The centre line divides the mass of the stone in half. If a platform is above the centre line, it is very likely the stone will break when you apply a force. If the stone doesn't break, you could end up with a lopsided item. If it is on or below the centre line, the flake should travel well without breaking the piece you are working on.

- **The angle of the force applied** With direct percussion the angle of the blow is more than 90 degrees in relation to the platform surface if a hard hammer is used (like a glancing blow). When using pressure flaking, or applying direct percussion with a soft hammer, the force is directed into the stone, following the direction of the flake you want to detach.

- **Flakes love to travel far over convex surfaces** They don't travel over concave surfaces, where they will just break off.

- **Flakes love to follow mass** They travel well along ridges and lumps on the stone.

MAKING A CHOPPER

1 Using a hard hammer, it is possible to create a rough tool such as a chopper in only three steps. Select a hammer stone and a flint nodule (the "core").

2 Flakes are removed by striking the edge of the core with sharp, forceful blows. The control of each blow is more important than its strength.

3 The rules described in the box above will help you predict where the flakes will come off, allowing you to shape the stone just as you want it.

Working with bones and sticks

Once your basic requirements of shelter, warmth, food and water are taken care of, you can use all the natural materials around you to create numerous other artefacts. If you are surviving in the wilderness for a long period you will want to make your life as comfortable as possible. You'll have time to develop your skills and to seek out the best materials for each task.

MAKING BONE TOOLS

The bones of any animals you kill for food should always be cleaned and saved for future use. Bone is soft enough to be shaped with stone, but hard enough to hold a sharp edge or point, so it can be turned into many useful tools, such as needles, fishing hooks, drills and punches. Large bones and antlers can be used for digging and hammering, or sharpened to make saws and knives.

Bones can be broken up easily by simply smashing them with a piece of rock, although the results may be unpredictable. If you want a specific shape, you can score bone in much the same way as glass to make it break in more predictable patterns. You can then give the bone its final shape using a fine abrading stone.

Bone tools can be extremely sharp. You can prepare an item such as a bone knife or arrowhead for sharpening by rubbing it with hot oil, then heating it in the fire. If you then sharpen the object much as you would sharpen a steel knife, you can get very sharp edges indeed.

BACKRESTS AND MATS

A simple backrest can make life a lot more comfortable, enabling you to relax in front of your fire or sit up in your shelter. You can make one quite easily using stout sticks arranged in a tripod. This will be easy to move around and stable on uneven ground.

You can make your backrest even more comfortable by weaving a grass mat to lay over it and sit on. You could also make a mattress to sleep on. For these you will need a lot of tall grass or long hollow reeds and a lot of cordage. Just keep adding more bundles of grass until you have a mat long enough for your needs. Its width will be decided by the length of the grass, though you can chop off the sides when you have finished if they are too long.

MAKING A KNIFE FROM BONE

1 Large bones, either found or harvested from an animal, can be broken up simply by smashing them with a rock to get shards.

2 Shape the resulting shards into whatever tool you need by using a large rough stone as an abrading block and rubbing the bone across it.

3 For greater precision, score the bone with a stone cutting tool in the rough shape of the object, then carefully "smash" it along the scored lines.

4 When the shaping of the knife is complete, rub hot oil into the bone, and heat the knife over the fire before sharpening the blade.

5 Sharpen the knife pretty much as you would a regular steel blade. Try to find a stone as smooth as possible for this sharpening process.

6 The bone blade can be bound into a notch in the end of another long, smooth bone or a piece of wood to create a handle.

MAKING A GRASS MATTRESS

1 Collect a large amount of long grass or hollow reeds. Start by making a bundle about 7.5cm/3in thick.

2 Split the bundle in half and turn one half over, so half the thicker ends are at each end, to keep the thickness even.

3 Tie the bundle using two or three long cords. Wrap the cord around itself three times to make each knot.

4 The knots provide a flat surface on which you can rest the next bundle. Tie this in using the same knots.

5 Repeat until the mat is the right size. The flat knots square off the bundles, eliminating gaps between them.

6 This method can be used to make mats of any size and shape you want. Trim the ends of the stems if you wish.

MAKING A BACKREST

1 Select three sturdy poles, each 90–120cm/3–4ft long. Make sure they are reasonably straight.

2 With the poles side by side, wrap a good length of cord fairly loosely around one end and knot it.

3 Wind the cord between the sticks to form a "cinch". This is the chance to tighten up your tie as much as possible.

4 When the top is tied securely, place the sticks upright, and bring the middle stick backwards.

5 Tease the two other sticks outwards to form a tripod. Adjust the distances between them to stabilize the structure.

6 Tie on some horizontal bars to give you a sturdy surface to lean against, and tie a grass mat over this frame.

Working with natural resins and oils

Both animal and vegetable products can be used to make glue, which has numerous uses in a survival situation. Apart from its use as food, animal fat is also useful as a lubricant, and can be used as fuel in lamps.

HIDE GLUE

Generally used to glue organic matter together, hide glue is the strongest glue known. The downside is that it stretches when wet, will not withstand heat, and will not glue materials such as stone. It is made from hide scrapings or pieces of rawhide, boiled until they dissolve into a thin liquid. You must use hide glue hot, as it sets fairly quickly on cooling. To reuse it, simply add a little water and heat it up slowly. However, it can be stored for only a few days before it goes off.

PITCH GLUE

The sap from conifers, chiefly spruce and pine, can be made into a good waterproof glue (it is used in the fishing spear project on pages 98–9). The resin seeps out of wounds on the trunks of trees, or can be found in blisters under the bark and scraped off with a stick.

Once you have a container full of resin, place it on the fire. As soon as it begins to melt, you will notice a strong turpentine smell: this is normal. Don't allow the resin to boil as that will reduce the quality of the glue. Make sure you have some sort of lid to hand as well, as it catches fire easily. If you have a large amount of resin, and require very clean glue, strain the liquid as quickly as possible, so it doesn't set while in the filter. For most outdoor projects, however, this is not necessary.

The resin on its own will simply revert to its natural state as it cools. In order to make it set hard and strong you need to add a "temper". Three different substances can be added, all with their own advantages. Powdered charcoal is most often used, because it's

MAKING HIDE GLUE

1 Place the scrapings from a hide in a fireproof container and pour on some water: you will need nine parts water to one part hide.

2 Put the container on the fire and allow it to boil. Fat may rise to the surface, and you should skim this off, but keep it safe.

3 Keep boiling, adding more water as required to stop all the moisture evaporating, until the hide has completely dissolved into a sticky glue.

MAKING PITCH GLUE

1 Collect a sufficient amount of spruce or pine resin in a fireproof container. Try to avoid getting too many little bits of debris mixed in with the resin.

2 Place the container on the fire and allow it to heat up. Keep stirring so that the heat is spread evenly and don't allow it to boil.

3 Mix in some powdered charcoal, wax or dried scat to make the glue set hard when it cools. Allow the liquid to set on sticks or in small clumps for storage.

MAKING AN OIL LANTERN

1 The container for an oil lantern can be made of many different materials. Pictured here are a simple clay bowl and a purpose-made lamp.

2 To render pieces of animal fat into usable lamp oil, heat it in a fireproof container on the fire, skimming off the liquid fat continually.

3 Pour this oil into the container you are using for your lantern. It is important you have rendered the oil well, so it remains liquid.

4 Make a "wick" for the lamp by braiding some plant fibres. The best fibres to use are from the resinous bark of trees such as red cedar and basswood.

5 Place the wick in the oil, making sure a little sticks out at the top. It is helpful to soak the entire wick in the oil for a minute or two to help it catch.

6 Now light the wick. The size of the flame can be adjusted to a certain extent by having more or less wick sticking out of the lamp.

easy to get. Charcoal works well for most purposes, though the glue may become brittle after a while. Beeswax creates a more flexible glue, though it is not so strong and tends to feel a little greasy. The glue also seems to be a little softer when set. A good temper is the dried scat of herbivores such as rabbits or deer, ground into a powder. This makes the strongest and longest-lasting glue, often referred to as "loaded" glue, though it is less hygienic – don't use it to waterproof a cup, for example.

It is hard to judge how much temper to add to the resin to make it set properly. Try about a tenth, then leave a little to set. If it sets hard, it's done. If it stays sticky and soft, add more. Once the temper is added, the glue must be used hot: it will set as it cools down.

It is best to divide the glue up into small portions containing just enough for each project. The reason is that the more times you re-heat the glue, the less strong and more brittle it becomes. There are many ways of dividing the glue into small portions, but the best is to create "pitch-sticks".

With a container filled with water to hand, take a small stick and dip it into the hot glue as you would dip a candle. Then place the stick with the blob of hot glue in the water to cool it down quickly. Briefly dip the stick into the glue again, so more glue is collected, and cool it again in the water. Keep repeating this until you have as much glue collected on the stick as you want. While the glue is still warm, you can mould it into raindrop or sausage shapes for easier storage.

When you wish to use the glue, you can either heat the object to be glued and touch the pitch-stick against it, or heat up the tip of the pitch-stick so that a drop of hot glue drips on to the surface of the object. You can improve the bond between the glue and the materials by pre-heating the surfaces to be glued.

OIL LANTERNS

The name would suggest that such lanterns use oil as a fuel. However, research into early societies has revealed that animal fat was often used for lighting. The oil lantern can be made from any container that will not burn. Clay containers are particularly good, because you can make them in any shape to suit your needs, easily creating a spout to support the wick.

The wick is best made from the bark of resinous trees such as red cedar and basswood. Alternatively, natural cordage made from nettles and other fibrous plants also works well. Simply melt the animal fat in the container and light the wick.

Index

Acknowledgements

The publishers and contributors wish to thank the following people for their time, expertise and contributions to the book. We sincerely apologize if we have omitted any individual(s).
Debra Searle (Veal) MBE and her sister Hayley Barnard at SHOAL Projects Ltd for providing the introduction and photographs http://www.debrasearle.com.
Helen Metcalfe for planning and shooting the photography sequences and **Bill Mattos** for modelling and providing models on those shoots – and also for providing many of the props for free. Both Helen and Bill are at Nookie Xtreme Sports Equipment http://nookie.co.uk/rescue.html.
Peter Drake for supplying the charts and African bushcraft photographs.
Mika Kalakoski for his help on snow shelters as well as supplying the snow

shelter images.
Rob Bicevskis for help on the images for making fire with a lens made of ice.
Tunde Morakinyo at the Iroko Foundation for supplying his jungle pictures.
Jean-Philippe Soulé at Around the World in a Viewfinder for the cahune palm shelter pictures – www.jpsviewfinder.com
With thanks to the following picture agency for the photograph they provided.
Alamy Images p18tr.

Patrick Mulrey for his invaluable survival step-by-steps and disaster scenario illustrations.
Peter Bull Arts Studios for the footprints, skining and tanning and hiding steps.
Sarah Ainley for her initial editorial setting up and input.
    Anthonio Akkermans would like to

dedicate his writing to Gillian and Reuben and to thank **Ofer Israeli** of Shomrei Hagan in Israel, who helped him with desert knowledge, guided him through the desert, and helped take the desert images.
Allan "Bow" Beauchamp: for some interesting discussions on primitive fire and also for images kindly supplied. **Tom Brown** and the instructors at the Tracker school for teaching these skills.
    Anness Publishing would also like to thank the following models for their time and effort under difficult and often treacherous conditions: **Garry and Loretta Harper, Matthew Harrison, Nikki Ball, Alastair Stewart, Paul Ross, Gabby Footner, Tattiana Cotts, S Atkins, Tim Denson, Alison Martin, Andy Parritt, Mike and Luke Waldock.**